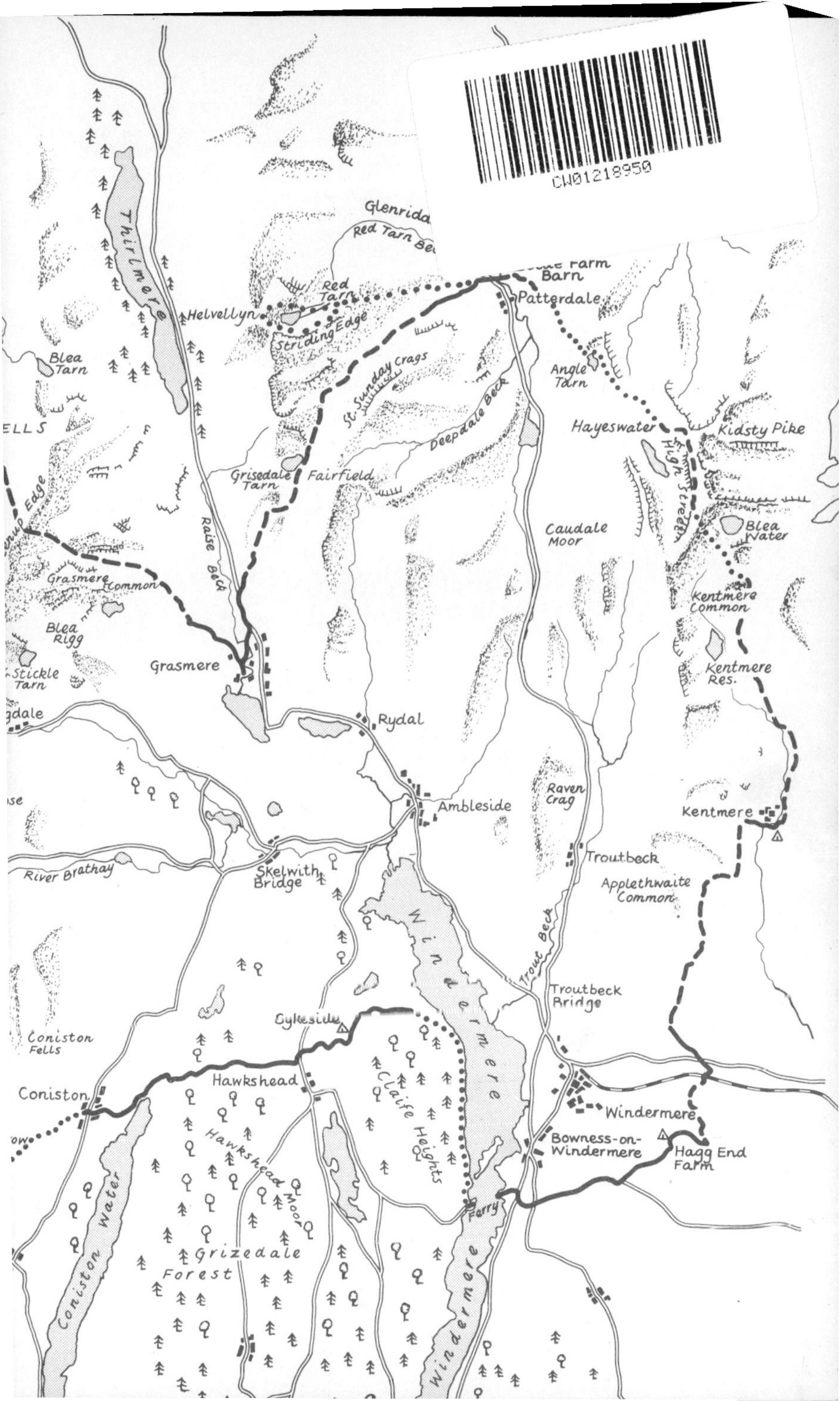
Thirlmere
Glenridd
Red Tarn Bec
Farm
Barn
Patterdale
Red Tarn
Helvellyn
Striding Edge
Blea Tarn
St. Sunday Crags
Angle Tarn
ELLS
Deepdale Beck
Hayeswater
Kidsty Pike
High Street
Grisedale Tarn
Fairfield
Edge
Caudale Moor
Blea Water
Raise Beck
Grasmere Common
Kentmere Common
Blea Rigg
Grasmere
Stickle Tarn
Kentmere Res.
gdale
Rydal
Raven Crag
Ambleside
Kentmere
Troutbeck
River Brathay
Skelwith Bridge
Applethwaite Common
Windermere
Trout Beck
Troutbeck Bridge
Sykeside
Coniston Fells
Hawkshead
Claife Heights
Coniston
Windermere
Bowness-on-Windermere
Hagg End Farm
Hawkshead Moor
Ferry
Coniston Water
Grizedale Forest
Windermere

Over the Fells

Over the Fells

Robert Orrell

Oxford University Press
Oxford   Toronto   Melbourne

Oxford University Press, Walton Street, Oxford OX2 6DP

London   New York   Toronto
Delhi   Bombay   Calcutta   Madras   Karachi
Nairobi   Dar es Salaam   Cape Town
Kuala Lumpur   Singapore   Hong Kong   Tokyo
Melbourne   Auckland

and associated companies in
Beirut   Berlin   Ibadan   Mexico City   Nicosia

Oxford is a trade mark of Oxford University Press

© text Robert Orrell 1984

All rights reserved. No part of this publication may be
reproduced, stored in a retrieval system, or transmitted, in any
form or by any means electronic, mechanical, photocopying,
recording, or otherwise, without the prior permission of
Oxford University Press

This book is sold subject to the condition that it shall not,
by way of trade or otherwise, be lent, re-sold, hired or
otherwise circulated without the publisher's prior consent
in any form of binding or cover other than that in which it is
published and without a similar condition including this
condition being imposed on the subsequent purchaser.

British Library Cataloguing in Publication Data

Orrell, Robert
Over the fells.
1. Lake District (England)—
Description and travel—
Juvenile literature
I. Title
914.27'804858   DA670.L1

ISBN 0 19 273152 1

Phototypset by Oxford Publishing Services, Oxford
Printed by Biddles Ltd., Guildford

*To Barbara
who loves the Lake District*

Illustration Acknowledgments

The publishers would like to thank the following for permission to reproduce photographs:

Geoffrey Berry, pp. 18, 31, 38, 83, 100, 101;
John Cleare, p. 23;
Bert Jenkins, pp. 71, 85;
Bob Orrell, pp. 16, 26, 32, 41, 47, 54, 58, 61, 64, 76, 88, 111, 116, 121, 124.

Acknowledgments

The author and the publishers are extremely grateful to the following suppliers, who generously provided equipment for the journey:

Field and Trek, Brentwood	Sleeping-bags, stove, water carrier, billies, compass
George Fisher, Keswick	Waterproof suits
Fjallraven, Harrogate	Kanken rucksacks
G. T. Hawkins Ltd, Northampton	Climbing boots
P. D. Hendren, Whitehaven	Photographic equipment
Marilyn Hutchcroft, Ennerdale	Handspun Herdwick sweaters
R. Saunders Ltd, Chigwell	Saunders Base Camp Tent

Grateful thanks also to Suc Cheesbrough for many hours spent typing the manuscript.

Chapter One

'This is a funny looking saddle,' exclaimed Philip, lifting the pack-saddle off the floor, 'where do you sit?'

'It's not for sitting on,' I said, 'it's a pack-saddle and it's only used for carrying things like boxes and bags. We're going to carry our camping equipment on it.'

'But what are all these straps for?' asked Abi, trying to sort out a tangle of harness.

'I can show you better tomorrow when we load Thor,' I said. 'It looks complicated, but it's quite easy to understand. Just stack it on the table for now. I want to check if anything is missing.'

The summer holiday was with us at last and for Philip and Abi it was to be a holiday with a difference. They had spent a lot of their spare time helping to look after my ponies and their parents had said I could take them with me on a journey through the Lake District.

At first my suggestion of a walking tour was greeted with groans and excuses.

'We live in the Lake District and can see it every day,' grumbled Abi. 'In any case, I can't possibly carry a rucksack, it makes by back ache.'

'I think I've sprained my ankle playing football,' said Philip, limping round the room. 'Look, it's swelling.' He waved his leg in the air, but before I could examine it he had hurriedly pulled his boots on.

'Oh well, we'll not bother then,' I said casually. 'It's just that I thought we might take Thor with us as a pack-pony to carry the tent and equipment.'

The response was electric.

'Take Thor as a pack-pony!' cried Abi. 'What a marvellous idea. I don't mind walking as long as I don't have to carry a heavy rucksack.'

Philip's eyes shone with excitement. 'I've always wanted to really explore the Lake District. We could follow the old smugglers' trails and try to find their caves.'

There was a mad scramble to find a map and spread it out on the kitchen table. 'We're here,' I said, pointing to a dot that marked my small farm at Gillerthwaite in the middle of Ennerdale Forest. 'We could follow the pack-horse route through the forest then climb over the fells by the passes and then, if you want to go along the smugglers' paths we could work our way to the coast at Ravenglass. We could go over the fells again to Coniston and across Lake Windermere by the ferry to the eastern fells at Kentmere and eventually make our way back to Ennerdale. What do you think of that?'

'It sounds fabulous,' said Philip, following the route on the map with his finger.

'How far will we have to walk each day?' asked Abi, cautiously.

'Oh, I think seven or eight miles a day will be enough,' I said. 'A lot depends on the weather, but we can always find a place to camp if you feel you're too tired to go on.'

Making a list of things we needed for the journey was great fun and the day before we were due to set off the kitchen floor was littered with the pack-saddle and harness, plastic bags bulging with breakfast cereal, packets of soup, dried potatoes, apples, oranges, cheese, sugar, lemonade crystals, chocolate, margarine, biscuits, matches and a first aid kit. Then there were sleeping-bags, foam rubber mattresses, a tent, knives, forks, spoons, cups, plates, pans and a paraffin stove. Abi had packed enough spare clothes for an expedition to the North Pole instead of two weeks in the Lake District.

'You can't possibly take all this, Abi,' I said, staggering under the weight of a bag full of what she insisted were 'essentials'.

'It's full of bath salts and tins of talcum powder to make her smell nice,' said Philip mischievously, 'all girls are like that.'

'No they're not,' retorted Abi, 'at least I'm not. I just like to be clean that's all.'

'You've got a tin of talcum powder in your bag, I've seen it,' taunted Philip. Abi went red and started to reply, but I interrupted. 'Would you two stop arguing, we've got a lot to do before morning. You can take one change of clothes each, two pairs of socks, a sweater, a towel and soap, a tooth-brush and paste and your waterproofs. And that's all, otherwise poor old Thor will be bow-legged before we've gone a mile.'

I picked up Philip's bag and felt the weight. 'What on earth have you got in here, a suit of armour?'

'It's only a book or two and a few comics to read when we're in the tent,' he muttered. Before I could put the bag down the seams burst with the strain and out poured six *Beanos*, five *Dandys*, four Enid Blyton books, a book about fishing in the Lake District, *How to Identify Birds*, *Know your Trees*, a book of ghost stories and *Swallows and Amazons*.

'Goodness me,' I gasped, 'he's a travelling library.'

Abi howled with laughter at the sight of the pile of books and comics on the floor. 'A bit heavier than a tin of talcum powder, aren't they Philip?' she teased between fits of the giggles. Philip bit his lip and looked downcast for a moment or two, but fortunately he saw the funny side of it and a broad grin spread over his face. 'Well, how much weight can Thor carry?' he asked.

'It depends on the type of country he has to walk over,' I said, 'but when we've loaded all our equipment on to him it will weigh about thirty-five kilograms, which is quite enough for any pony to carry over the fells.'

When the last item was packed into the three canvas bags which were to be tied to the pack-saddle and each bag carefully weighed with a small spring balance, we sat round the lounge fire and discussed our route.

'I think we'll have an easy day to start with,' I said, spreading the map on the carpet. 'We'll go through the forest and over Black Sail Pass to Wasdale and ask permission to camp at a farm. It's only a few miles and it will do nicely to loosen our muscles up. I'm going to give you a notebook and pen and I want you to keep a diary describing what we do each day. If we follow the tracks the smugglers used to take you'll have plenty to write about. I'd like you to list the birds we see along the way and also wild flowers and places of interest.'

Philip coughed. It was a signal he was about to ask a question. 'What is it now?' I asked, faking a yawn. 'If you're going to ask me can you take a giant telescope so that you can look at the stars, the answer is definitely no.'

'Er no, it wasn't that,' he said with a grin. 'Please can I take my fishing-rod, it's only short and I'll carry it on my rucksack.'

'He says he'll catch fish for us every day,' smirked Abi, 'but I'm glad we're taking food with us or we might get very hungry while we wait for a fish to jump on to his hook.'

Philip put his tongue out at her and, sliding the fishing-rod out of its narrow canvas bag, handed it to me. It was a nice little fibreglass boat rod in two sections, each about forty-five centimetres long and, together with a small spinning reel, it was an ideal rod to take on a camping holiday.

'It's a super rod,' I said, passing it back to him, 'but what are you going to catch with it?'

He picked up the copy of *Where to Fish in the Lake District* from the floor. 'If you'll let me take this,' he said eagerly, 'it tells you which tarns and rivers have fish in them, and if we camped by them I bet I could get a trout for breakfast.'

'All right, it's a bargain,' I said, 'you can take the rod and the book and we'll stop as often as we can.'

Abi was not convinced. 'I bet we have to buy a packet of fish fingers,' she grumbled.

Philip grabbed a sock and flung it at her.

'You rotten thing, what did you do that for?' she yelled.

'It's one way of telling you to put a sock in it!' said Philip, chuckling at his own joke.

I intervened before it developed into a full-scale battle. 'We have to be up early in the morning, so save your energy for the walk tomorrow. Off you go to bed. Breakfast is at eight o'clock sharp.'

Chapter Two

Early the following morning the sun rose slowly over the long ridge of Red Pike and High Stile, which forms a high barrier on the northern side of the Ennerdale valley. As it climbed higher into the pale blue sky, rays of golden light caught the tops of the peaks and painted them first a bright pink, then a deep red. The warm glow crept steadily down the rocky fellside and chased dark shadows between the rows of spruce trees in the silent forest.

'Isn't it beautiful?' exclaimed Abi. She was leaning on the yard gate with her chin cupped in her hands, staring spellbound at the view.

'Fantastic,' spluttered Philip, as he staggered across the yard, weighed down by the heavy canvas bags. At least it sounded like 'fantastic', but the word was lost. He was carrying his fishing-rod in his teeth at the same time. Dropping the bags on to the ground, he collapsed on top of them. 'Phew,' he exclaimed, mopping his forehead with his sleeve, 'if it's hot this early, what's it going to be like later on.'

'Hotter,' giggled Abi.

'All right, clever,' retorted Philip, 'stop daydreaming and come and help me to carry the bags out, we're leaving soon.'

'Coming,' called Abi slowly, and continued to stare into space over the gate. Philip waited for a second or two, but she ignored him. 'Girls!' he snorted and stamped back to the house.

After breakfast, Thor was brought up from his field and given a thorough grooming with a stiff brush. Of all the ponies on my farm, Thor is my favourite. He is a typical fell pony, black, with short stumpy legs, a large friendly face and a long mane and tail. He much prefers eating and sleeping to anything else and has to be coaxed into action with lumps of mint cake. He is slow when going downhill and painfully slow when going uphill. He is frightened of tractors, absolutely hates anything that flaps in the wind and is positively terrified of mice. But he does like apples and boiled sweets, people who give him titbits and anyone who is prepared to spend hours untangling knots in his mane.

'Why do we have to do this?' Abi panted with the effort of pulling the grooming brush along Thor's broad back. 'He looks clean enough to me.'

'Well look at it this way,' I replied, 'if you got out of bed in the morning and went out for the day without having had a wash or combed your hair, you'd probably feel very grubby and uncomfortable. It's just the same with a pony. Besides, you have to make sure his hair and skin are clean before you put a saddle on him, otherwise he'll become very sore.'

Philip dumped the pack-saddle and harness on a bench by the barn door and looked puzzled. 'I still can't understand what all these buckles and straps are for,' he said. I lifted the pack-saddle and placed it on Thor's back. 'Well, imagine a load fastened to the saddle. As long as Thor is walking along a flat path the saddle will stay in the middle of his back. But if we were climbing a steep path the saddle would slide down his back and fall off, so a wide piece of leather called a breast-strap is fastened round his chest. And if Thor were going downhill the saddle would slide over his head, so to hold it back straps called breeching fit round his back legs under his tail. If everything fits properly a pack-pony can go up and down hill all day without the pack falling off.'

With the pack-saddle and harness carefully placed in position, the bags crammed with equipment were tied on to the saddle with rope, one on each side and one resting across the top. A quick check was made to see that the load was well balanced and we were ready to start. To hold our waterproof suits, notebooks, maps and bars of chocolate for lunch, we each carried a small rucksack.

Sensing we were about to leave, my Border collie, Sammy, went wild with excitement and rushed about barking furiously. Philip laughed, 'He wants to come with us, can we take him?'

Ready to leave — the start of the journey at Gillerthwaite

Sammy dropped a stick at my feet and looked up with large, brown eyes, begging me to say yes.

'Well all right,' I said, 'on condition that you'll look after him and keep him on a lead when we go through farms and villages.'

Philip raced back to the house to fill a bag with dog food. 'I'll look after him, I promise,' he shouted.

Abi untied Thor's lead rope from the post. 'Can I lead him through the forest?' she asked.

'All right,' I replied, 'but walk to one side of him or he might stand on your heels.'

Abi pulled gently on the rope and Thor lumbered through the gate on to the wide forest track. We were on our way. Abi leading Thor, Philip and I a few metres behind, and Sammy racing in front to find a stick. There was hardly a cloud in the sky and it was very hot as we plodded slowly along between the rows of tall spruce trees. After an hour or so I called a halt and we rested in the shade of a huge heap of logs stacked by the side of the track and let Thor nibble at the few blades of grass growing out of the bank.

'Does all this wood go to make paper?' asked Philip, sucking noisily on an orange.

'Most of it,' I replied, 'although these long, thick tree trunks which we're sitting on will be sawn into boards and lengths of timber for building houses. If you look at the thin end of each log you'll see that it's marked with numbers. The one next to you is marked six point three and fifteen; it simply means that the log is six point three metres long and it is fifteen centimetres in diameter at its narrowest end. From those figures a forester can tell how much money the log is worth.'

'That's a good idea,' said Philip. 'I'm going to look for the biggest log in the forest as we are walking along.'

Pillar Rock and Pillar Mountain

We continued for over four miles, following the track as it climbed steadily upwards through the trees towards Great Gable blocking the head of the valley. At times the track went right along the edge of a gorge and we looked down a tremendous drop to the River Liza, thundering and crashing over the rocks below. At a point where there was a wide gap in the trees, Philip suddenly stopped, open-mouthed. 'Hey, look at Pillar

Rock,' he called, pointing upwards. Abi and I joined him and we looked up through the trees. A vast, rocky pinnacle towered above the forest, filling the whole skyline like a huge church spire. The sun was shining on it and every rock face and grassy ledge stood out, crystal clear.

'Gosh!' exclaimed Abi. 'I've never seen it so clear. I wish we could climb it.'

'Well, we might one day, but one step at a time. We've got this journey to do first. Let's move on.'

At the edge of the forest we joined an old pack-horse track and followed it for a mile or so to Black Sail Youth Hostel, one of the remotest hostels in the Lake District. Many years ago it was a shepherds' hut, where they lived during the summer months, looking after their sheep on the high pastures, but it was eventually taken over by the Youth Hostels Association. The Warden was out when we knocked, but the door was open and, full of curiosity, Abi and Philip had a quick look inside. Sammy sneaked round the back to see if there might be a bone lying about, but he came back looking very disappointed. All around the hostel the scenery was magnificent, with tremendous peaks and towering crags in every direction. From the hostel door we could see Black Sail Pass very clearly, zigzagging up to a ridge between Kirk Fell and Pillar.

'Have we got to go up there?' Abi couldn't believe it. 'It looks far too steep to take a pony. Can't we go round?'

Philip bit his lip and looked worried, but said nothing.

'Don't worry,' I said, 'it's not as bad as it looks. Hundreds of pack-ponies used to go over the Pass in the old days, carrying wool from the farms, and smugglers came this way too, with ponies carrying barrels of rum and whisky, so I think old Thor will climb it without much trouble.'

I took Thor's rope and led the way along a narrow path from the Youth Hostel to a wooden bridge crossing the River Liza. Thor snorted and refused to step on the bridge at first, but we fed him with lumps of Kendal Mint Cake and he was so busy chewing he forgot to be frightened and walked across without hesitating. From the bridge the path climbed easily at first, then steepened as we reached the foot of the Pass. It was still incredibly hot and sweat poured off us with the exertion of climbing only a short distance. We rested briefly, then started the long slog up a very rocky path winding up the fell. Years of heavy rain had washed the surface away and Thor had to clamber up tricky patches of rock right on the edge of a long drop into the beck below. Philip and Abi watched anxiously as he slipped and skidded, sparks flying from his iron shoes, but they need not have worried; Thor was a native pony of the Lake District and used to rough ground. As we climbed higher, Black Sail Youth Hostel shrank to the size of a doll's house, far below, and we had a marvellous view right down Ennerdale. Abi was wheezing like a leaking balloon by the time we reached the half-way mark and Philip's face was the colour of a beetroot.

'Shall we give Thor a rest?' I said, when we reached a wide ledge.

'Oh yes please,' croaked Abi, 'I'm dying for a drink.'

'Me too,' whispered Philip hoarsely, and sank against a boulder.

Luckily we were not far away from a small beck and we filled our cups with ice-cold water mixed with orange crystals. It was absolutely delicious. Thor slurped his ration out of a soup bowl, but Sammy decided the best way to cool off was to jump in the water instead of drinking it and he wallowed and splashed like a baby seal. For once we did not mind when he shook himself and sprayed us with a cold shower.

At the top of the Pass we rested again and basked in a refreshing breeze blowing inland from the coast. The first section of the long descent into Mosedale was extremely steep and loose and I had to guide Thor down it very slowly to prevent him from slipping over the edge. All was going well when suddenly one of the straps on the breeching snapped under the strain and the loaded pack-saddle slid down on to Thor's neck. He tried to lift his head but the weight of the packs held it down and he began to panic. Abi grabbed one side of the saddle and Philip the other, while I tried to push it along Thor's back, but it was too heavy. Slowly the weight began to drag him towards the edge of the path and a steep drop, and although we pulled desperately, trying to hold him back, it was pulling us as well. Thor had almost reached the edge when I managed to release the girth straps and the pack-saddle thumped on to the rocks. Abi heaved on Thor's lead rope and pulled him to safety while Philip jumped on the pack-saddle to stop it rolling down the fell.

'That was a close thing. Are you two all right?' I asked anxiously. But they were none the worse for the fright and a piece of chocolate kept Thor happy while we struggled to strap the saddle on to his back and lash the bags into place. Lower down the fell the path improved and we made good progress down a long series of zigzags to Mosedale and followed a good path to Row Head Farm. Mr Naylor, the farmer, said he did not allow camping on his land, but when he saw we had a pony with us he said we could stay for one night and showed us a small paddock with plenty of grass.

'I hope that dog is safe with sheep,' he grunted, looking at Sammy.

'Yes,' I said, 'he's very well trained, he's a working sheep-dog.'

'Is he now,' he said, fondling Sammy's ear and opening his mouth to look at his teeth. 'He's not very old, but he's certainly a handsome fellow.'

Sammy looked pleased and licked his hand to show he wanted to be friends.

We pitched the tent in the corner of the paddock and, having turned Thor loose and stowed all the gear in the tent, we walked through the fields to the Wastwater Hotel to quench our thirst with glasses of iced Coca Cola. We were ravenously hungry when we returned and hurriedly prepared a meal of beef chow mein followed by a mug of Oxo. Sammy crunched his dog food then lay down in a corner of the tent and fell fast asleep.

Walking at a steady pace it had taken us until 6 o'clock to reach Row Head Farm and now, as the evening advanced, dark shadows were creeping over the head of the valley. We sat in the grass outside the tent and watched the last rays of the setting sun flicker across the craggy face of Great Gable.

'Look at that. It's like a searchlight,' said Abi excitedly, as a ray of light swept down Great Hell Gate Screes and lit up the vast rock buttress of Eagles Nest Ridge. Philip dived into the tent for my binoculars and managed to scan the crag before the light faded.

'What did you see?' I asked as he pushed the binoculars back into their case.

'I thought I saw something that looked like a huge spike of rock at the bottom of the crag, but I'm not sure.'

'It's a spike of rock all right,' I said. 'It's the most

Great Gable behind Wasdale Head Farm, showing Napes Ridge and Crags

famous spike of rock in the country. It's called Napes Needle and it's very impressive when you're standing close to it. It's about thirty metres high.'

'I'd love to see it,' said Abi. 'Can we climb up to it tomorrow?'

'We can if you really want to,' I said, 'but it's quite a slog to reach it and it means asking the farmer if we can stay another night. What about you Philip, do you want to climb up to the Needle?'

'Oh yes please,' he said without hesitation, 'I've always wanted to try rock scrambling and I could make a sketch of it in my notebook.'

'All right then,' I said, 'you get into your sleeping-bags and I'll go and ask the farmer if we can stay another night.'

When I returned, ten minutes later, they were both fast asleep.

The next morning the lovely blue sky had vanished and thick cloud hung over the fell tops. It was still very warm though and we ate our breakfast by the edge of a beck that flowed past our campsite. By nine o'clock we had washed up, tidied the tent, checked the paddock gate to make sure Thor could not get out and, with Sammy on a lead and rucksacks well filled with chocolate bars, apples, cameras and films, we set off through the farmyard and joined a well-trodden path leading towards Great Gable. For the first half mile or so the path was easy but, crossing a wooden foot-bridge, we reached the foot of Great Gable and started up an incredibly steep path leading across scree to the base of the crags. We had already climbed quite a way up the fellside, but to reach the Needle we were faced with a difficult scramble over loose boulders and stones.

'I hope you've got a good head for heights,' I called, working my way along a particularly nasty section of the path, only wide enough for a boot and with a sheer drop to the valley below. 'Make sure you've got a firm grip and you'll be all right.' I let Sammy off his lead and he ran off in front of us.

Abi edged her way slowly across, followed by Philip, and we scrambled up to the safety of a broad, grassy ledge below a wide expanse of grey rock.

'I can't see Napes Needle,' said Philip, staring at the

crags in front of us.

'Be patient,' I said, 'we're not quite there. This is the start of Eagles Nest Ridge, the Needle is just round the corner.'

A wall of rock barred our way and forced us to descend a rib of loose stones and heather to the foot of a broad gully and there we saw it. High in the gully, carved by nature out of solid rock and standing vertically, like the head of a gigantic spear, was Napes Needle. Forgetting the danger of the drop below us, Abi and Philip stared, wide-eyed at the sight of this unique rock.

'Has it ever been climbed?' said Philip.

'Oh yes, hundreds of times', I replied, 'but it was a chap called Haskett-Smith climbed it first, nearly a hundred years ago. What makes it particularly difficult is that there is no easy way off the top and you have to be an experienced rock climber before you can tackle it.'

We climbed the gully to the foot of the Needle and stared at the smooth walls. 'Well, now you've come all this way to see it, would you like to climb a little way up it?'

'Can we?' they chorused in amazement.

'There's a ledge about seven metres up,' I said, 'it's quite safe and the climbing is easy.'

'Oh great,' shouted Abi and swarmed up like a monkey. Philip's legs were shorter than Abi's and he could not reach some holds, but by standing on my shoulders he managed to get a grip and heave himself up to join her. Sammy was determined not to be left behind and tried to jump up to the ledge, but I made him guard the rucksacks and he whimpered with frustration as we climbed the rock and left him behind.

Two young rock climbers, festooned with rope, scrambled up behind us and prepared to climb a ridge

Abi and Philip on Napes Needle

close to the Needle.

'I think I would like to be a rock climber,' said Abi as the climbers sorted out their ropes and equipment.

'I wouldn't,' said Philip, 'this is quite high enough for me.'

We watched the climbers work their way up the steep ridge, protecting each other with the ropes as they went, until, with a wave, they disappeared out of sight over the top of the crag.

Sammy was overjoyed to see us when we climbed down the Needle to the gully and retrieved our rucksacks and he raced ahead as we followed a high path right across the face of Great Gable to an old pony track at Sty Head. It was late in the afternoon, but it was still very hot and we lay in the heather by the edge of a tumbling beck and drank mug after mug of cool water laced with lemonade crystals. From our vantage point we could pick out the route of the pony track winding its way down the fellside to cross Lingmell Beck by a ford, then making almost straight for the inn at Wasdale Head.

'Did the smugglers use this pass as well as Black Sail?' asked Abi.

'Yes,' I said, 'it was used a great deal. In fact, in its day this was part of the main route from the port of Ravenglass to Keswick. They used to smuggle all sorts of things, but because the Sty Head route drops down into Borrowdale it was used for smuggling something rather unusual and I bet you can't guess what it was.'

'I know. Home-made whisky,' said Philip.

'No. I'll give you a clue: it's used in pencils.'

'In pencils,' said Abi, disbelievingly. 'What would they want to smuggle pencils for?'

'Well they didn't actually smuggle pencils,' I said, 'but the black lead inside them. There used to be a black lead mine at Seathwaite in Borrowdale a long time ago and, in those days, black lead, or "wad" as the locals called it, was nearly as valuable as gold. The owners used to have armed guards patrolling near the mine, but they weren't clever enough to beat the smugglers. They used to take it to Ravenglass and exchange it for brandy and French lace smuggled in from the Isle of Man.

'It would be fun to follow the same path as the smugglers when we set off tomorrow,' said Philip, busily writing about black lead in his notebook.

'And go to Ravenglass, to see where they landed their ships,' added Abi.

'Well we will, if the weather keeps fine,' I said. 'We'll go over Burnmoor and down Mitredale to Ravenglass. But come on,' I jumped to my feet, 'Sammy is getting impatient. Let's go back to the campsite.'

It was nearly seven o'clock when we reached the tent and we were tired and weary. Thor was stretched out in the grass, fast asleep, but he woke up with a snort when he heard us and trotted over to see if there was any Kendal Mint Cake to spare. We were ravenously hungry and feasted on fried sausages mixed with instant potatoes and baked beans; it looked revolting but tasted marvellous. As darkness approached, huge black clouds drifted down from the fell tops and drove all the warmth out of the air.

'It looks as if there's a storm brewing,' I said, as I looked through the tent door and watched Kirk Fell and Great Gable being slowly swallowed up by the cloud. 'I think we ought to pile stones round the edge of the tent and on the tent pegs in case there's a gale in the night.'

Abi and Philip were in their sleeping-bags and were very reluctant to leave them, but when I pointed out that to spend a few minutes gathering stones would be much better than having to climb out in the middle of the night to hunt for missing tent-pegs, they were out in a flash and carrying stones from the beck.

Chapter Three

During the night there was an occasional rumble of thunder, but when daylight came the sun appeared from behind the clouds and bathed the valley in a warm glow. After breakfast we dragged everything out of the tent and carefully packed the holdalls, weighing them to make sure they would balance evenly on Thor's back. At nine o'clock we left the field and called at the farmhouse to thank Mr Naylor for allowing us to camp. He had been up early gathering sheep and the yard echoed with a constant baaing and bleating as ewes looked for lost lambs among the seething mass of woolly bodies. We stopped to watch the men as they grabbed a struggling sheep then, holding it firmly between their knees, skilfully removed the fleece with electric shears. A dab of red marking fluid was brushed on its side and it was released into a pen, looking very embarrassed about being made to stand around without any clothes on. Sammy whimpered with excitement and longed to leap in and show how he could gather sheep and keep them in order, but Philip kept him on a tight lead.

Abi led Thor through the yard of the Wastwater Hotel then, by way of a shallow ford, over Lingmell Beck to the National Trust's campsite on the edge of Wastwater. Almost every tent seemed to have a radio blaring away and the noise made Thor very nervous.

'Keep a good grip on his rope, Abi,' I warned.

'Thank goodness we didn't have to camp here,' she said. 'We wouldn't have been able to listen to the birds or the sheep or anything.'

Sammy growled his disapproval and kept close to my heels. It was a relief to leave the noisy campsite behind and join a track slanting across the fellside above Wasdale Head Hall Farm. The surface of Wastwater was like a mirror and as we climbed higher the view was absolutely breathtaking. Wasdale Head was laid out below us like a relief model in a geography class. Green meadowland was divided into squares, rectangles and circles by the grey stone walls. Tiny cattle and sheep grazed close to the miniature farmhouses and model cars stood in rows in front of the white painted inn. Only the high fells that enclosed the head of the valley in the shape of a horseshoe were as tall as we were and we could see over the bristly ridge of Yewbarrow to Red Pike and the long, flat summit of Pillar. Close to Pillar was Kirk Fell, looking for all the world like a circular pyramid with a pointed top. Even our old friend Great Gable had lost its rugged appearance and looked like an upturned pudding basin decorated with pebbles. While we rested we spent a few minutes practising map reading and Abi became quite excited when she discovered that we were on the lower slopes of Scafell.

'It's a pity we can't go to the top, then I could boast that I've climbed the highest mountain in England.'

'Well you'd be wrong,' I said. 'Scafell Pike is the highest.'

'But I always thought Scafell and Scafell Pike were the same,' said Philip.

'So do a lot of people,' I said, 'but if you look at the map you'll see that although they stand next door to each other, they are separate summits.'

Scafell Pike (centre) and Scafell (right) from Wastwater

'So they are,' said Abi, kneeling over the map spread on the grass. 'Scafell Pike is nine hundred and seventy-seven metres and Scafell is nine hundred and sixty-four metres. Oh well,' she went on, 'I don't care, it's just as nice being on the second highest.'

Thor had found a juicy patch of bleaberries while we were studying the map and refused to leave when we wanted to set off again, but a prod on his rump and the promise of a lump of mint cake when we reached the top spurred him on. The angle of the track eased off on the crest of the ridge and ahead was the bleak expanse of Burnmoor. Abi led the way, guided by cairns of stones placed at intervals among the banks of slimy peat. The track was difficult to find at times, but eventually we reached hard, dry ground and from the top of a little hillock we looked down on the glittering waters of Burnmoor Tarn. Philip hurriedly produced *Where to Fish in the Lake District* from his rucksack and thumbed through the pages.

'Listen to this,' he said, and read from the book in an urgent voice, as if he had discovered some top secret information. '"Burnmoor Tarn contains a variety of freshwater fish including Brown Trout."' He thrust the book back in his rucksack. 'Can we stop while I fish for a bit?' he pleaded. 'I bet there's some real whoppers in there and I might get one or two for tea'

'All right then,' I said. 'You agreed that if I let you bring a fishing-rod you would provide us with fresh fish, so now you've got a chance to prove it.'

'Oh, no, surely we're not going to waste time fishing,' cried Abi, 'he never catches anything.'

'I do so,' said Philip, huffily. 'I've caught lots and I'll catch one or two here, you'll see.'

'Humph!' said Abi.

When we reached the tarn I slackened Thor's girth strap and let him graze on the few patches of grass by the water's edge. Philip quickly assembled his fishing-rod and reel and tied on a few hooks and a bright orange float. Sammy sat beside him, head cocked on one side, fascinated by this new game.

Waiting for a bite

'Stand back, I'm going to cast,' hissed Philip, 'and you mustn't make a noise.'

We ducked as the line swished round our heads and watched the float sail through the air and land with a plop in the water. In a flash Sammy realized what the orange thing was. Of course, it was a ball! With a loud yelp he plunged into the tarn and, grasping the float in his teeth, swam back to the bank and dropped it at Philip's feet, shaking himself vigorously and spraying icy water all over us. Philip was absolutely furious.

'Sammy, you great stupid idiot,' he yelled, 'you've frightened all the fish away now. Go and lie down.'

Poor Sammy slunk away and cowered in the heather licking his paws. Philip angrily sorted out the tangle of line and float and, placing fresh bait on the hooks, he cast the line again. For over an hour he tried several different places around the tarn, but without success. He was terribly upset and hardly spoke as he unscrewed his rod and put it in the canvas bag. 'That book is a lot of rubbish,' he muttered, swinging his rucksack on to his shoulders and stamping off along the track.

For once Abi realized he was in no mood for jokes and tried to cheer him up. 'Never mind, you'll be able to fish in the sea when we reach Ravenglass,' she said comfortingly. Philip perked up at the idea.

'Great,' he exclaimed, his face breaking into a big grin. 'I might land a salmon.' He patted Sammy's head, 'Sorry I shouted at you, Sammy.' Sammy wagged his tail and bounded away to find a stick for Philip to throw for him.

Leaving the wide pony track, we followed an easy path west, by the deserted house of Burnmoor Lodge, then across open moorland to descend steeply into the wooded valley of Mitredale. Most of the cloud cleared from the sky and it was very hot. We stopped briefly to drink from the ice-cold water of Black Gill, then pressed on through Low Place Farm to join a surfaced road leading to Irton Road Station on the Ravenglass and Eskdale miniature railway. A train arrived while we were crossing a humpbacked bridge over the line and the hissing and clanking of the steam engine gave Thor such a fright he ran off up the lane. When we eventually caught up with him he was standing in a field up to his knees in buttercups, chewing happily with a herd of cows. He was very reluctant to leave his new friends and Abi had to heave on his rope before she could lead the way through a mass of prickly gorse bushes to a good path leading to Muncaster Fell and Ravenglass.

Compared with the fells around Wasdale, Muncaster Fell is not very high, but the view from it is one of the best in the Lake District. From the summit, not only can you see many Lakeland peaks, but also the hills of Southern Scotland and the Cumbrian coast from St Bees Head, round in a wide curve, to a large fell called Black Combe, above the town of Millom. If the weather is particularly clear you can see well beyond Black Combe to Morecambe Bay and the Lancashire coast.

'Is that the Isle of Man?' called Abi, standing on top of the summit cairn and pointing to what looked like a huge, upturned boat lying on the surface of the blue Irish Sea.

'Yes, you're quite right,' I said. 'That's the summit of Snaefell sticking up in the middle.'

'Isn't that where those fish called kippers come from?' asked Philip. He seemed able to think of nothing but fish.

'Well a kipper isn't exactly a fish itself,' I explained. 'It's a herring that's been opened out and smoked over a wood fire. Because the Isle of Man fishing fleet catches a lot of herring, the islanders have built up a kipper smoking industry and they send them all over the country.'

'We have them for tea sometimes,' said Abi. 'They taste delicious, but I wish they'd take the bones out.'

We dropped down from the summit and continued along the path, carefully avoiding patches of oozy peat and sphagnum moss.

'What on earth's that?' said Abi, pulling Thor to a halt and staring at a large slab of rock resting on two smaller boulders at the side of the track. Philip dashed ahead to get a closer look.

'It's got letters and figures on it,' he shouted. 'Do you think it was a place where Druids used to sacrifice human beings?'

'Ugh! I hope not,' said Abi. 'The thought gives me the creeps.'

'Look at these marks on top of the rock. I'll bet they were made by the points of swords when they were pushed through girls being sacrificed,' said Philip fiendishly.

'Stop it, you bloodthirsty little horror,' squealed Abi, backing away from the rock and looking as though she was about to run all the way to Ravenglass.

'Ignore him Abi,' I said. 'He's got a vivid imagination, but he couldn't be further from the truth. You've only got to look at the date carved on the rock to realize that.'

Abi peered cautiously at the rock. 'Ross's Camp 1883,' she read out. 'Was it an army camp?' she asked.

'No,' I replied, 'though there's an interesting little story behind it. Ross was the estate manager for Lord Muncaster of Muncaster Castle at Ravenglass and he liked the view from here so much he had a wooden chalet built so that he and his family could stay for several days. Why he brought this huge stone here no one really knows, but a farmer friend of mine in Eskdale told me that it used to be in the yard of Hinning House Farm, that's the farm below us,' I said, pointing to a whitewashed farmhouse in the valley. 'My friend's grandfather lived at the farm and he said that Mr Ross hired a team of six Clydesdale horses and hauled the stone to the site of his chalet and a stonemason carved his name and the date on it.'

We set off again and dropped down the fell to the tiny village of Ravenglass where we camped for the night in a field near the beach. While Abi and I erected the tent, Philip hunted for worms on a smelly dung heap by a ruined barn.

'I've got some beauties,' he shouted, brandishing a squirming heap in a plastic bag. 'There's bound to be plenty of fish in the sea. I'll be back shortly.' And clutching his fishing-rod, he dashed down the lane to the beach. He was away about half an hour and when he returned he was clutching a large fish.

'Goodness me, Abi,' I said, jumping to my feet, 'he's caught one already. It's fish for dinner tonight.'

Philip dropped the fish on a plate, but far from being excited about his catch, he was surprisingly silent.

'What's wrong?' I asked. 'Are you worn out with the effort of landing the monster?'

'No,' he muttered, turning red in the face.

'What then?' I persisted.

'Er, well, I didn't actually catch it,' he confessed ruefully. 'The tide was out, so I swapped my bag of worms for the fish with a man working on a boat.'

We looked at him in amazement, then burst into fits of laughter.

'That's brilliant,' cried Abi. 'I would never have thought of that.'

No meal of fish and potatoes ever tasted as good as dinner that night and all for the price of a bag of worms!

Chapter Four

It was a flock of herring-gulls arguing over the skeleton of our fish that woke us early the next morning. They were perched on top of a wall and made the most awful din, squabbling and swooping at each other in an attempt to fly off with the fish bones.

'Go away, you noisy brutes. Shoo, shoo!' shouted Abi, crawling through the tent door and waving her sweater at them. They rose in a cloud of flapping wings and flew away over the village. 'What a gorgeous morning,' called Abi. 'Come and look at the sea.'

Philip and I pulled on our boots and scrambled out of the tent. The grass was still wet with the morning dew and we kicked up clouds of spray as we ran across the field to the shingle beach. Abi was right, it really was a beautiful day. The tide was coming in fast and the wavelets breaking on the beach flashed and sparkled in the bright morning sun. Ravenglass is a natural harbour formed by three rivers, the Esk, the Mite and the Irt, joining together in front of the village and flowing out in a narrow estuary to the Irish sea. On either side of the estuary are miles and miles of golden sand dunes that are the home of black-headed gulls and colonies of oyster catchers. Many other birds and animals live on the sand dunes but not a solitary thing moved as we stood staring at the deep blue sea and listening to the sound of the advancing tide as it swirled around our boots.

On one side of Ravenglass's only street the houses reach out into the estuary

'What a smashing place for smugglers to land their boats,' said Philip. 'I wonder if there are still rum barrels and other things hidden in the sand dunes. I wish we could explore them.'

'Well it's quite possible that some stuff might have been buried and forgotten,' I said, 'but there's not much chance of finding anything. In any case, the smugglers would only leave their cargo in the sand dunes until it was safe to bring it into the village. Come on, I'll show you one of the houses where they used to hide it.'

We walked along the beach to the edge of the village street and stopped at the rear of an old house which had a flight of stone steps leading up from the beach, but ending mysteriously at a blank wall.

'This house used to be called the Ship Inn,' I said, 'and according to some old tales, was a favourite smugglers' hide-out. Some say the Customs men forced the landlord to brick up the door at the top of the steps to stop smugglers sneaking in during darkness.'

'Gosh, it must have been really exciting being a smuggler,' said Philip. 'Did they ever get caught?'

'I suppose they must have done at times,' I replied, 'but they had very fast sailing-ships and they knew every inch of the coast.'

We left the old Ship Inn and spent an hour or so wandering round the picturesque cottages in the village's only street, before loading Thor and setting off through the grounds of Muncaster Castle, heading for Eskdale. It was fiendishly hot once we left the shelter of the tall trees around the castle and climbed the steep fellside. In many places the path was overgrown with thick bracken, almost as tall as Thor, and it took ages to force our way through it.

'It's hard to believe this was once a Roman road,' I panted, smashing down the bracken with a heavy stick and heaving fallen branches to one side. 'It was the Romans who first discovered Ravenglass and then cut this road through to Eskdale to build a fort on Hardknott Pass, but they would have a job getting through it nowadays.'

I dragged a heavy tree trunk to one side and the worst was over. The path descended steeply through Chapels Wood and on the way passed close to an attractive stone tower. We stopped to look inside. Sammy had exhausted himself chasing rabbits, so we left him with Thor, dozing under the shade of the trees.

'Was it a watch-tower of some sort?' asked Abi. 'It's got slits all the way round to fire arrows out of.'

'It looks as if it was part of a castle at some time,' said Philip, peering inside the door, 'but there's no sign of any steps leading to the top.'

'Well, it's got quite an interesting history behind it,' I said, 'but it wasn't a watch-tower or part of a castle. It was built as a monument to King Henry VI, who was

King of England in the fifteenth century. You might not have covered the Wars of the Roses in your history lessons at school yet, but it was a long conflict between King Henry, who was from Lancashire and whose emblem was a red rose, and the Duke of York, whose emblem was a white rose. In a battle at Hexham, in Northumberland, King Henry was beaten, but managed to escape and hide in the hills. The story goes that two shepherds were working with their sheep in the field where we are standing now, when a man appeared and asked the way to Muncaster Castle. He was covered in mud and absolutely worn out. The shepherds took him to the castle and the Lord of the Manor, Sir John Pennington, discovered that the traveller was King Henry himself. He stayed at the castle for a few days and when he left, the King gave Sir John a small glass bowl and said the Penningtons would always have good luck, provided the bowl was never broken. The bowl is still in the castle today and the Penningtons built this tower to mark the spot where the shepherds found the King.'

'What a lovely story,' said Abi, 'but what happened to King Henry after he left the castle?'

'Ah well, it's rather a sad ending,' I said. 'He reached Lancashire safely, but he was betrayed and captured and eventually died in the Tower of London.'

'That's awful,' said Abi, 'and after all he'd been through, too. Let's leave him some flowers.' And flinging her rucksack on the ground, she gathered a bunch of foxgloves, field daisies and buttercups. 'There you are King,' she said quietly, placing the flowers on a ledge inside the tower, 'that's from us.'

Below the tower the path joined a wide track and we followed its winding course up Eskdale until it joined a surfaced road by the King George IV Inn. It was so hot hardly a word was spoken as we trudged along the hard,

Monument to King Henry V1, known locally as Chapels Monument because it is in Chapels Wood

dusty track, and the sight of the inn was like a mirage in a desert.

'Please could we stop and buy a glass of orange?' said Philip hoarsely. 'My tongue feels like a piece of leather.'

'Mine too,' said Abi. 'I could drink a whole lake.'

I bought four large glasses of orange squash, one for

each of us and one to share between Thor and Sammy. Feeling a lot better, we rejoined the old Roman road at Forge Bridge and followed it through lush, green meadows, along the edge of the River Esk, to the welcome shade of Scots pine and oak trees in Dalegarth Wood. Thor's hooves and our boots scarcely made a sound on the carpet of soft soil and leaves and there was an almost eerie silence as we threaded our way between the shadowy trees.

'Isn't it spooky,' said Abi with a shiver. 'I'm glad I'm not on my own. I get the feeling that robbers are going to ambush us at any minute.'

'Oh, you're safe enough these days,' I laughed, 'though it might have been different a hundred years or so ago, when pack-ponies came this way, loaded with all sorts of valuable goods. An old man in Ravenglass once told me that his great-grandfather used to bring a lot of cattle this way too. Ships brought them to Ravenglass from Scotland and the Isle of Man and drovers took them over the fells to the market at Kendal. It was a long, hard walk for the cattle and to stop their feet being damaged on the rough ground a blacksmith used to shoe them, just like a horse.'

After a mile or so the dark canopy of leaves and branches thinned out and the sun streamed through shimmering silver birch and bright green larch trees. On we went, passing Dalegarth Hall, with its peculiar round chimneys, and winding in and out of woods and meadows, until eventually we reached Penny Hill Farm, near the head of the Eskdale valley. The farmer's wife was very friendly and helpful and obtained permission from the owner of a nearby estate for us to camp in a small field by the edge of the River Esk. We were so hot and dusty we flung our boots and socks into the grass and raced down the field to soak our feet in the cool water. Sammy dived straight in and swam round, barking excitedly to us to join him. Thor rolled contentedly in the grass for a minute or two then ambled after us and stood in the river, sucking noisily at the water and blowing it through his teeth like a great black hippopotamus. When the tent was pitched and the equipment neatly stowed away under the flysheet, I rummaged through the food bag.

'What would you like for dinner?' I asked.

'Ugh, I can't bear the thought of food,' said Abi. 'It's far too hot to eat. All I want is a cold drink.'

'I'm not hungry either,' murmured Philip, stretched out in the grass. 'Let's mix a panful of water and orange crystals.'

'You've got to eat something, we've got a long way to go tomorrow. How about sardines?' I held up a tin.

'Ooh, no thanks,' said Abi, pulling a face.

'I don't like sardines,' said Philip. 'If we've got to eat I'll just have a few biscuits and a piece of cheese.'

The evening meal was a very sparse affair, but the heat certainly did not affect Sammy's appetite. He pulled his bag of dog food from under the tent and sat by it wagging his tail until I poured a heap on to the grass.

When the sun went down in the evening, we sat on a little hillock above the campsite and watched the fells change colour and the trees lose their shape as dusk settled over the valley. Beautiful though it was, there were very obvious signs of a change in the weather.

'Look at the fells,' called Philip, 'it's so clear you can almost see every rock.'

'It's nice to look at,' I said, 'but it could mean the end of the sunny days. Look at the clouds forming.'

High in the sky a strange bank of cloud, broken up like huge, flat snowflakes was creeping in from the west.

'It's a sure sign of a change in the weather when you

can see a long way and that type of cloud comes across the sky. We'd best make sure everything is under cover.'

'Does that mean we're in for a storm?' asked Philip, fearfully.

'Oh no,' I smiled, 'nothing as drastic as that, but make sure your waterproofs are easy to get at when we set off tomorrow.'

It was so hot and humid during the night it was impossible to sleep and by eight o'clock the next morning we were dressed, packed and ready to leave. The weather was still fine, but the cloud that was creeping in when we went to bed had now completely covered the sky and had turned from fleecy white to a threatening grey. A few spots of rain thudded on to our backs as we followed the bridle-way through Penny Hill Farm towards the bulk of Harter Fell. At the foot of the fell a great wooded chasm carries Spothow Gill, a normally placid beck that splashes its way over a rocky bed to join the river Esk. During heavy rain though, the beck swells to a mad, raging torrent, which over the years has ploughed through rocks and boulders and swept away the ford where, at one time, the packmen and cattle drovers were able to cross without difficulty. Nowhere could we find a crossing place for Thor and we floundered around in chest high bracken until we found what appeared to be a path leading down to the road at Wha House Bridge. We eagerly followed it only to find our way barred by a single strand of wire.

'Don't touch it,' I yelled, as Philip and Abi walked forward, 'it's an electric fence.'

They both jumped back in horror.

'We might have been electrocuted,' gasped Abi, 'they ought to be banned.'

'Oh it won't hurt you,' I laughed. 'It works off a battery and the idea is to give cows a slight shock to stop them from straying. Come and help me to move it.'

We gingerly untied the string holding the wire to a tree and, while I held it to one side, Abi led Thor through the gap and Philip scurried after them leaving me to retie the string. Heavy drops of rain bounced off the leaves of the trees as we reached Wha House Bridge and the surfaced road leading to Hardknott Pass. We were heading for an old pack-horse track which starts at the foot of Hardknott Pass and traverses diagonally across Harter Fell to Dunnerdale. By the time we reached it the drops had become a downpour and we scrambled into our waterproof coats and trousers and pushed on up the steep track, panting with the effort of trying to keep up with Thor. There were many stops to get our breath back before we reached the top, but eventually the worst was over and we sat on a rock and looked down through the sweeping rain to the glistening valley below. On the move again, the wide track ended in a sea of bog, but a thin path led us safely through to the edge of Dunnerdale Forest.

It was still very warm, despite the rain, and conditions were perfect for that nasty little brute the midge to come out and look for breakfast. In the Lake District, the midge lives in boggy ground and damp woods, not in ones or twos, or in tens, or even hundreds, but in thousands. They delight in annoying humans and when they saw us arrive at the edge of the forest they descended in a huge cloud and crawled over our faces, into our ears and hair, noses, mouths, up our sleeves and down our shirts, until there was hardly an atom of skin that was not covered in red blotches. No amount of arm waving would dislodge them, but fortunately they hate the dark and finally we managed to escape from the little pests by plunging deep into the forest. An hour of tripping over hidden roots and falling into holes full of water and black slimy peat brought us to the edge of the forest and an isolated farm at Grassguards, perched high on the fellside above Dunnerdale. The rain was pouring down like a monsoon and the air had turned very chilly.

'Could you drink a mug of soup?' I shouted, as we slipped and slithered down through the trees to a gate.

'Oh yes, please,' shivered Abi. 'But where can we shelter from the rain?'

'We'll find a big tree with lots of branches. I'll go on ahead. Philip, follow me with Thor, will you.'

Quite close to the farm I found a huge Sitka spruce and soon we were huddled together under the branches with a pan of soup bubbling on the stove. Sammy curled up between us and went to sleep and to keep Thor happy, Abi gave him a packet of biscuits. As we sipped our soup and stared at the rain bending the branches of the smaller trees around us, Philip started laughing to himself.

'Isn't it silly,' he giggled. 'Only yesterday it was so hot we couldn't eat and now we're shivering with cold and having hot soup.'

'Well, that's typical of the weather in the Lake District,' I said, 'and it's one of the reasons why so many people get lost on the fells. They look so easy to climb when the sun is shining, but in mist and rain they can become very dangerous.'

'I think I prefer the woods to the fells,' said Abi. 'You can shelter from the sun if it's too hot and sit under the trees and have soup if it's raining.'

Thor was dozing peacefully under another tree when I tied the bag containing the food and stove back on to the pack-saddle and he was rather grumpy about having to move on again. We tempted him with a large piece of

'Is it ready yet?' — Lunch break in the rain at Grassguards

mint cake and he crunched it loudly as we descended a steep, rocky path to Dunnerdale, to a series of large stepping-stones crossing the wide River Duddon. A wire rope stretched above the stepping-stones provided added safety and Abi and Philip skipped across while I coaxed the reluctant Thor to wade into the water. We were glad when the rain eased to a drizzle. Just above the river we joined a motor road when I let Thor graze while we ate chocolate and studied the map, looking for a place to camp.

'How are you both feeling?' I asked.

'A bit tired,' said Philip, 'but I'll go on for a while yet.'

'Me too,' said Abi, 'although if we could find somewhere to camp I'd like to change into dry clothes, the rain has seeped through my anorak.'

'All right,' I said, 'we'll stop the night in Dunnerdale

and tomorrow we'll go over the Walna Scar road; it's a very old pack-horse track leading from Dunnerdale to Coniston. The map shows a farm called Long House at the foot of the Walna Scar and it will be a good point to start from. Let's ask if we can camp there.'

It took several minutes of loud knocking on the farmhouse door before heavy bolts were drawn back and the farmer's wife stood on the threshold.

'Would it be possible to camp on your land for the night and graze our pony?' I enquired.

'I'm very sorry,' the farmer's wife replied, 'I'd like to help you, but the owner of the farm will not allow us to take campers. You could try further down the valley, though I'm not sure if they would take your pony.'

It was a dreadful let-down, but there was nothing we could do but apologize for troubling her and lead Thor back up the farm track to the road. Abi and Philip looked very miserable and weary and to add to our problems a strong wind sprang up and drove vicious gusts of rain on to us.

'We've got two alternatives,' I said, as we crouched in the shelter of a wall discussing what to do. 'We can walk down the valley to another farm, but if they won't take Thor we're really stuck. On the other hand we're right at the foot of Walna Scar now and if you're game we can carry on over the top to the old mine workings at Torver, where we can camp on the fellside. I'd better warn you though, it's a fairly tough walk and the weather is getting worse. What do you say?'

To my astonishment they never hesitated.

'Let's carry on. We're thoroughly wet now,' said Abi, 'so we can't get much wetter.'

'I'd rather continue than risk being turned away from another farm,' said Philip.

'That's very brave of you,' I said. 'We'll wait until

this squall blows over then we'll set off.'

When the wind died down I checked Thor's girth and the packs and led the way to the foot of the Pass. Years of rain, snow and frost had long since gouged away the original surface of the track and we alternated between walking along a rocky trench and wading ankle deep in mud. At times it was very strenuous and our bodies were soon steaming with the effort of having to lift our mud caked boots high enough to continue walking. Half-way up the fell the track passed through a gate in the wall and I was leading Thor towards it when Philip shouted, 'Look behind you! We're in for it now.'

I glanced over my shoulder to see an enormous black cloud tearing towards us, spreading out across the sky and plunging the valley into darkness.

'Quick,' I bellowed, 'get through the gate and behind the wall.'

We ran as fast as our mud caked clothing would allow and collapsed behind the wall in the nick of time. With a roar like an express train, the wind hit the wall, bringing with it torrential rain that churned the track into a sea of mud within seconds. Stinging hailstones lashed through gaps in the wall and thudded into our anoraks like bullets. Sammy flattened himself against us, whimpering with fright as the wind howled and screamed overhead. Thor was terrified and tried to run away, but I kept a firm grip on his rope and pulled his head behind the wall. It was an incredibly nasty squall, yet as quickly as it came, it went, raging across the fell towards Coniston. Within minutes the wind had dropped and the heavy rain died away to a drizzle.

'Wow,' said Philip, shaking the white layer of hailstones off his coat, 'I hope we don't get caught in another one of those while we're climbing the Pass.'

'So do I,' said Abi. 'That was really scary.'

Leaving the shelter of the wall, we trudged slowly on up the track. Looking down on Dunnerdale, the scene was breath-taking. A weak sun had somehow managed to squeeze its face through the cloud and the valley shone like silver as shafts of bright light swept across the saturated fields and swollen becks. Then, as if someone had turned off a light switch, the valley was plunged into semi-darkness again as another belt of advancing cloud swallowed up the sun.

'That cloud looks as if it's heading this way,' I warned. 'Fasten your coats securely and tie the cords of your hoods to stop the ends from hitting you in the face.'

We were only a short distance from the top of the Pass when the squall caught up with us and a sudden gust of wind bowled Philip completely over. He quickly scrambled to his feet and hung on to the pack-saddle. All the way to the summit of the Pass we were battered and buffeted by the wind and rain and as we squelched past the summit cairn the wind increased to gale force. But we were safely over. The wind realized it had lost its battle and, with a final blast that blew my woolly hat off my head, it retreated to Dunnerdale and left us in peace to look down on a sunlit valley, as if we had crossed into another world. On the Coniston side of the Pass the track had been so badly washed out it was impossible for Thor to walk on it and, at times, I had to lead him down steep heather. Far below I could see the tempting expanse of grass where I hoped to camp, but it never seemed to draw any nearer as we made long detours to avoid nasty drops. It took ages before the final awkward section of path was over and the last slippery slope was behind us. We had made it. With a tremendous sigh of relief we pitched camp close to a fast flowing beck and dived inside the tent for a huge dinner of soup and corned beef, followed by biscuits and jam.

Camping in open country with a pony is always a problem. Unless they are fenced in, most ponies will wander in search of food and can often be a very long way from the campsite the following morning. To prevent Thor from wandering when we pitched camp, I fastened hobbles to his front legs. These are simply two broad leather straps joined together by a short chain which, when fastened round a pony's front legs, allow it to move very slowly and prevent it from straying. At least that is what hobbles are supposed to do, but it is amazing how a clever pony can devise ways of escaping. When we started our dinner Thor was grazing happily by the tent, but by the time we had finished he was nowhere to be seen.

'He's disappeared,' said Abi, having searched the area around the tent in a wide circle.

'Rubbish,' I retorted irritably. 'How can a great oaf like Thor disappear? He's probably asleep in the long bracken. Have another look.'

Philip joined Abi and they set off to search a jumble of old buildings near the campsite. Taking binoculars, I climbed a nearby hill and scanned the horizon, but there was no sign of life. Suddenly a familiar whinny rang out over the fellside and Thor appeared from behind a wall, shooting along in a series of great leaps. He had discovered a way of moving forward even with the hobbles and he was on his way back to Ennerdale.

'Catch him,' I yelled, and Abi raced through the bracken and grabbed his headcollar while he was taking a breather.

'Thor, I'm ashamed of you,' I scolded when Abi and Philip brought him back to the campsite. 'You've had an easy time so far and in another week or so we'll be home. We're doing this journey and we need your help.' He stood with his ears back, listening to me, but I am sure he would have run away again given the chance. To make it difficult for him to escape, I tied a piece of rope between his headcollar and the hobbles to prevent him from lifting his head and leaping forward. He tried a few times but eventually gave up and, sinking into the bracken, he fell fast asleep.

During the evening the sky darkened ominously and thunder clouds growled at each other as they swirled around the dark crags above our campsite. A fierce wind whined through the bracken, flapping the canvas of the flysheet and straining the guylines. It was a sure sign of an approaching storm and, piling rocks on to the tent-pegs, we snuggled deep into our down sleeping-bags to escape from it. Sammy sensed something wrong and burrowed under my sweater, leaving only the tip of his tail peeping out of a sleeve. The first spots of rain thumped against the tent about midnight and within seconds a heavy downpour was battering the canvas as if we had camped underneath a waterfall. All night the storm raged with squall after squall doing its best to tear the tent to pieces. We could not sleep and we lay with sleeping-bags pulled over our heads listening to the wind approaching first with a slight whisper as it swished across the fellside, increasing to a moan as the rain squall gathered speed, then finally a screaming roar as it reached us with full fury. Abi and Philip were worried that the tent might blow down, but when I convinced them it was made to withstand storms, we passed the long night playing spelling games.

Chapter Five

The first streaks of dawn broke through the clouds at around five o'clock in the morning and I unzipped the tent door and looked out. It was an incredible sight. Water was cascading off every fellside and huge waterfalls poured down the crags, sending boulders and debris crashing in watery avalanches through the bracken. By eight o'clock the rain and wind had died away and the air was so warm we were able to eat breakfast outside the tent. There was no sign of Thor and for a horrible moment I thought he had run away again, but Philip found him sheltering under an overhang of rock. Thunder was still rumbling round the fell tops and, anxious to be on our way before another storm caught us, we dragged all the gear out of the tent, only to have to hurl it all back in again and dive after it when a heavy shower poured out of the sky without warning. It cleared away after ten minutes or so and we clambered out to strike camp and load Thor.

We joined a broad, stony track and followed it round the base of a large, straggling fell, until it merged with a surfaced road that dropped steeply to the village of Coniston. It began to rain heavily as we approached the village main street and we stopped in the doorway of a hotel to put on our waterproofs. Thor decided he liked the look of a large plant inside the hotel and gave the guests a dreadful fright by clattering up the stone steps and pushing the door open.

'A horse', gulped the manager, hardly able to believe his eyes. Then recovering quickly, he shouted, 'There's a horse standing on my new carpet, get it out, get it out!'

A burly porter strode across the hallway, but by this time I had a firm grip on Thor's lead rope and heaved him out of the hotel and down the road. The street was crammed with visitors and cars and we threaded our way carefully through them to the safety of a small patch of grass by the village car-park. An 'Ice Cream' sign attracted Philip's attention and he dashed across to a shop and returned with four large cornets. Quite a crowd of amused onlookers gathered when Thor started to eat his cornet. He is a terrible show-off and makes all sorts of funny noises when he eats ice cream.

In the centre of the patch of grass there was a stone monument with a plaque and Abi and Philip wandered over to look at it.

Donald Campbell Memorial Plaque

'"In memory of Donald Campbell C.B.E.,"' read Abi, '"who died on January 4th 1967 while attempting to raise his own world water speed record on Coniston Water."'

'I've never heard of Donald Campbell,' said Philip, 'who was he?'

'Oh, he was famous for attempting speed records in cars and boats,' I said. 'His boats and cars were always called *Bluebird* and, in fact, he reached over 400 miles an hour in his car.'

'Golly!' exclaimed Philip. 'That's faster than some aeroplanes. What speed did he do in his boat?'

'Well when he came to attempt to break the water speed record on Coniston in November 1966, he already held the world record at over 276 miles per hour and he wanted to try for 300. On the day mentioned on the plaque, January 4th, 1967, he tried early in the morning and reached 297 miles per hour and decided to have another run and see if he could go over 300. There were a lot of people watching and I was there myself, standing on top of a hill above the lake. I saw the boat speed down to the lower end of the lake and then turn and rest for a few minutes. Then with a tremendous roar of its engines, it started off again, but when it reached about half-way up the lake I saw it fly into the air and crash down on the water and sink.'

'How terrible,' said Abi. 'Did they manage to find it?'

'Yes, they found the wreckage of the boat in very deep water and a little doll he carried with him as a mascot was floating on the surface, but although they searched for weeks, they never found Donald Campbell's body.'

Abi and Philip hardly spoke a word after we left the monument and splashed through the rain towards

Hawkshead. Even when I suggested stopping for hot soup they showed little enthusiasm.

'Look,' I said after a long silence, 'there's no point in brooding about Donald Campbell. He knew what risks he was taking and I'm sure he would have no regrets.'

'Do you think so?' said a whispered voice from deep inside an anorak hood.

'I'm sure of it, so stop upsetting yourselves and let's shelter in the wood ahead of us and make a pan of soup.'

It was rather uncomfortable sitting in the rain, heating soup on the paraffin stove, but it was worth the effort. We felt a lot warmer when we set off again to climb the long hill out of Coniston. The narrow road was very busy with cars and as each one whizzed by we were sprayed with small stones and icy water. To make matters worse the rain came down in such torrents we could hardly see ahead of us, but we stumbled on until we reached the top of the hill and escaped into a lay-by. We ached in every bone, but the rain had not finished with us yet. It brought a strong wind along to help it and we were blown down the last few miles to Hawkshead with such force we were almost running.

On the edge of the village a car stopped and a friend of mine, Jean Crosbie, climbed out to talk to us. She insisted that instead of camping we should spend the night at her house and she would dry our wet clothes. It was an offer not to be refused and we pushed on through the rain to Sykeside, an old farmhouse hidden in a wood not far from the edge of Lake Windermere. Jean and her husband, David, were waiting for us with a meal and a huge log fire roaring in the sitting-room. The driving rain had seeped into our anoraks through zip-fasteners and we were soaked to the skin. Jean rummaged through her cupboards and lent us an assortment of shirts and trousers while our wet clothes were spread out to dry in the kitchen. It was absolute bliss to relax in dry clothes and bask in the warmth.

The rain cleared away completely during the night and early next morning the rays of the sun streamed through the windows and promised a fine day. Feeling refreshed with all our clothes dry, we thanked the Crosbies and set off in warm sunshine to walk a mile or so to High Wray and the start of a wide track running between plantations of tall trees on the shores of Lake Windermere. What a contrast to the previous day; the sky was blue and all around us the aroma of pine and spruce and peaty soil hung in the warm air.

'We haven't used our wild flower identification book since we started our journey,' I said, 'let's see if you can identify a few flowers on the side of the track. What about these tall red plants here?'

Abi rummaged through her rucksack and brought out the small *Oxford Book of Wild Flowers* and she and Philip stood in front of the plant and attempted to identify it.

'I can never understand these books,' grumbled Philip. 'It's full of pictures but where do you start looking?'

Abi was busy reading the introduction. 'It says here that the flower drawings are divided into colour sections so if we look at red flowers we'll probably find it.' She thumbed through the pages. 'Oh dear, there are dozens of red flowers, it will take ages.'

'Hey, stop there,' said Philip, peering over her shoulder, 'that looks like it.'

Abi turned back a page or two, '"Rosebay willowherb,"' she read, 'yes, that's it. We've found it.'

Inspired with the success of identifying the first plant, they hunted along the hedgerow and discovered herb robert, bistort, dog rose and speedwell and argued over several more. Thor rather spoilt the fun by eating

'I wonder what this is called?'

the flowers as soon as they were identified so we put the book away and continued through the wood.

'Can we stop for a while so I can fish?' pleaded Philip, as the winding path took us close to the water's edge. I had almost forgotten he was still carrying his fishing-rod.

'All right,' I said. 'We'll stop for an hour and have a picnic. Is it worth getting the frying-pan out?'

Philip went red in the face, but ignored the taunt and, emptying his fishing tackle on to the ground, started to fit it together while Abi and I unloaded Thor and tethered him to a tree on a long rope. It was a perfect day for fishing, but Philip's chances of catching anything were spoilt by an inconsiderate family in a speedboat, who kept zooming up and down, sending a tremendous wash up the beach. No self-respecting fish could be expected to tolerate treatment of that sort and they all swam off to another part of the lake. At least I imagine that is what happened because, even after an hour of patiently casting his stale crust of brown bread into the water, not a solitary fish was tempted to nibble at it.

'When I grow up I'm going to ban speedboats,' said Philip threateningly, thrusting his fishing-rod into its bag. 'Some people just don't care.'

'Never mind,' I said, attempting to cheer him up, 'let's go for a swim.'

At the word 'swim', Sammy raced down to the lake and jumped in before we had time to take our boots off. Abi said she would paddle instead of going in for a swim.

'You're frightened of showing your skinny legs,' jeered Philip splashing water at her.

'No I'm not,' she snapped, 'and if you really want to know, I've got quite nice legs. It's just that it's too hot for swimming.'

But Philip was not listening, he was racing Sammy to an abandoned ball floating on the water. The sun had climbed high into the sky and it was such a delight to sink into the cool water and escape from the sweltering heat. It was mid afternoon before we loaded Thor and continued on our way along a thickly wooded shoreline at the foot of the steep scar of Claife Heights.

'What a super place to camp,' said Abi, gazing longingly at a lush, green meadow reaching down to the lake edge.

'It looks tempting in daylight,' I said, 'but I don't think you'd be very keen to stay at night; it's haunted by a ghost called the "Crier of Claife".'

'Ugh,' shivered Abi, 'I can't bear the thought of meeting a ghost, let's move on.'

'They don't scare me,' boasted Philip. 'What sort of ghost is it?'

'Well, that's the weirdest part of the story,' I said, 'because no one who has met it has lived to describe it. It all started on a stormy night a few hundred years ago. Just a little way ahead of where we are now is the ferry which carries cars and passengers across the narrowest part of the lake, but in those days the ferry was a rowing-boat and anyone wanting to cross had to shout for the boatman. Well, on this particular night, there was a terrible storm raging and the boat was tied up on the other side of the lake by the ferry house and the boatman was sitting by his fireside feeling sure that no one would want to cross on such an awful night. Just about midnight, he was preparing to go to bed when he heard a voice shouting from the other side for the boat. He wasn't keen to row across in such rough conditions, but it sounded as though the person needed help, so he pushed his boat into the water and set off. He was away a long time and when he returned he was alone and whatever he had seen was so horrifying he was struck dumb with fright and died a few days later. From that time, whenever the weather was stormy on the lake, shouts and screams could be heard coming from Claife Heights.'

For once Philip was lost for words. He had listened to the story with wide eyes and his mouth open.

'Gosh,' he gulped, glancing nervously at the shadowy woods, 'perhaps we ought to get going. I'm sure Thor is keen to reach a farm,' and grabbing the lead rope he led the way along the track to the ferry.

The modern car ferry, which hauls itself back and forward across Lake Windermere on wire ropes, was unloading on the opposite side when we arrived and it meant a wait of twenty minutes or so. We were ravenously hungry and joined the queue in front of a mobile snack-bar and tucked into hamburgers, ice cream and coke. When the ferry arrived the ferryman very kindly held the cars back until Thor was wedged safely in a corner of the deck and, though he snorted with fear at first, he soon calmed down when he found he was the centre of attention, with children crowding round to pat his nose and feed him biscuits and sweets. The ferry chugged across the lake and grounded gently on the opposite bank where we joined a slow moving crocodile of vehicles as it crawled along the narrow road leading from the ferry. At a T-junction the cars turned off towards the town of Windermere, leaving us to plod slowly up a long hill and escape into a quiet lane overhung with shady sycamores and bordered with scented hawthorns and hedgerows of red campion. We were dripping with sweat and longing for a cool drink by the time we reached an isolated farm at Hagg End where I asked if we could camp for the night. A girl called

All at sea! — On the Windermere ferry

Tanya, who helped to run the farm, showed us to a patch of soft grass in the shade of a wall, and we were so tired within half an hour we had pitched the tent and were fast asleep inside it.

The next day was as beautiful as any day could be. Early in the morning a white mist hung over the field where we camped, but as the sun rose higher it warmed the air and the mist vanished, revealing a pale blue sky and a marvellous view over bright green meadows to purple fells in the distance. Tanya came to ask if Abi and Philip would like to learn to milk a cow and we all went with her to the byre where Daisy, a fat brown and white Ayrshire, was already chomping through her breakfast. Tanya sat on an old three-legged stool and slid a bucket under Daisy's bulging udder.

'Now, milking is quite easy if you think about it,' said Tanya. 'Those four teats are full of milk and to get it to flow into the bucket you have to squeeze them firmly, not pull down on them.' She demonstrated by gripping a teat between her thumb and forefinger and squeezing. A jet of milk squirted into the bucket. 'To do it properly, you sit right up to the cow, grip the bucket between your ankles and tilt it slightly. Then using both hands, grip the two teats nearest to you and squeeze alternately, like a pumping action.' She demonstrated and a continuous stream of milk frothed into the bucket.

'Doesn't it hurt her?' asked Abi.

'Not if you do it right, and Daisy would soon let you know if she wasn't happy. Come and try it.'

Abi sat on the stool and nervously gripped a teat with one hand. She squeezed several times, but nothing happened. Daisy stopped eating and turned her head to see who the unfamiliar hand belonged to.

'Try again,' said Tanya, 'but this time move your

hand higher up and if you press you'll feel the milk flowing.'

Abi squeezed and this time a few drops of milk splattered into the bucket. She tried again and within minutes was milking with both hands, as if she had been doing it all her life. When Philip tried he never quite mastered the technique, but he managed to get a pint or so before Daisy bellowed a warning that if he did not squeeze more gently she would kick him into the yard. To be on the safe side Tanya finished milking her and took the full pail into the house to filter it through a special sieve. Then there were calves to feed, byres to muck out, eggs to collect and a whole host of other jobs to be done every day, no matter what the weather was like. Sammy was overjoyed when a flock of sheep had to be moved from one field to another and he wriggled through the grass on his stomach to show Tanya's dogs that he, too, was a real sheepdog and not just a pet. It was late in the morning before the last tasks were finished and, reeking strongly of cow dung and sheep, we waved our thanks to Tanya and were off down the farm lane towards the hamlet of Ings and a pony track that would take us over the fells to Kentmere.

It was another hot day and Thor sweated so much the pack-saddle kept slipping to one side and threatening to fall off. It was infuriating to have to adjust it every ten or fifteen minutes and eventually we rested and let Thor dry off in the sun. There was no hurry, it was only a short distance from Ings to Kentmere and we lazed in the heather by the edge of a beck and drank lashings of ice-cold water. Abi found an attractive clump of flowers growing in the ruin of an old building and with the help of our flower book we identified them as great hairy willow herb. With the pack-saddle

Approaching Kentmere Hall Farm

buckled into position again on Thor's broad back, we continued along a dusty track with a superb view over the Kentmere valley to the high fells and the Nan Bield Pass, which we planned to climb the next day. Philip borrowed my binoculars and scanned the route over the Pass.

'It looks steep,' he said, 'I hope Thor will be able to climb it.'

'You needn't worry about that,' I replied, 'as long as the weather is good, he'll bound up it like a sheep.'

Dropping gently down to the valley, we reached the end of the track in the yard of Kentmere Hall Farm and stopped to admire the old building.

'Was it a castle at one time?' asked Abi, busily making a sketch of a square tower attached to the farmhouse for her notebook.

'Well, not exactly a castle, it was just a tower the owner of the land and his family could take refuge in when the Scots came into Cumbria to raid farms and drive the cattle back over the Border. Eventually, when the raids stopped, farmhouses were built and there's an interesting tale about Kentmere Hall. Most old farmhouses have a huge wooden beam above the fireplace which supports the floors above and when they were building this farm the beam was so heavy not even ten men could lift it. While they were struggling with it a man called Hugh Hird, from Troutbeck, the valley on the other side of the fell, came to see if he could help. He was called the "Troutbeck Giant" because of his size and he just picked up the beam on his own and placed it in position on the walls. The beam was about ten metres long and if you think about it, that's the length of a bus.'

Philip paced out ten metres along the track while Abi made a sketch of Hugh Hird holding the beam above his head.

We were given permission to camp in a field close by the River Kent and as soon as Thor was unloaded we changed into swimsuits and plunged into a deep pool. At first the cold water took our breath away, but we spent the afternoon having great fun sliding down a waterfall and diving under the water. Sammy had a whale of a time diving in to retrieve sticks and racing round to slide down the waterfall. When we tried to lie in the sun to dry off, he shook water all over us until we were forced to join him in the pool again. The swim gave us an enormous appetite and for dinner we had large helpings of mashed potatoes and sausages, followed by cheese, biscuits and fruit cake. When the pans and plates were washed and put away, I spread the map out to decide on the next day's route.

'We've got a tough day ahead of us tomorrow,' I said, 'so we'll have to make an early start. We've got about ten or twelve miles to cover, which may not sound much, but it will involve a lot of fairly strenuous climbing before we reach the summit of High Street. As you can see from the map, it's eight hundred and twenty-eight metres high and quite a long walk to reach it. On the top we follow the summit ridge and then descend by way of the Knott and Satura Crag to Angle Tarn, then down to Side Farm in Patterdale. If we half fill the water-carrier we can either drink the water or make soup, depending on what the weather is like. I'd like to leave here by nine o'clock at the latest, so I suggest we have an early night.'

There was a rush to spread out mattresses and sleeping-bags and, although we lay and watched the sunset through the open tent door, we were all fast asleep before the sun finally slid down behind the fells and darkness settled over the peaceful valley.

Chapter Six

The following morning a heavy dew clung to the branches of the trees and hedgerows as we led Thor through the field gate and on to the road, but when we climbed above the hamlet of Kentmere the sun had already dried the grass. It was a glorious morning, fresh and clear, and the view was delightful, with green pastures and wooded slopes spreading out on either side of the valley and reaching up to the sharp ridges and peaks of the high fells. Walking on soft, springy turf was a welcome change from the hard, dusty surfaces we had experienced and we were constantly stopping to identify wild flowers. There was bright yellow tormentil, sweet smelling wild thyme and delicate blue harebells, but the best find was clumps of tall yellow plants called monkey flower, growing in wet ground by the edge of a beck. Kentmere seemed to be a naturalists' paradise and at every bend we discovered new plants or stopped to watch crows feeding on a dead sheep, or kestrels hovering above the stone walls, waiting patiently for a shrew to scurry through the grass. From a safe branch in a high tree, a buzzard watched warily as we approached and, not quite sure what to make of us, flapped its powerful wings and glided away across the valley.

The climb up Nan Bield Pass was steep and rough at first where the original path had been washed away and Thor had great difficulty keeping his feet on the loose shale and clay that crumbled under his weight. Higher up, the angle eased off, but the path had been cut across the side of a steep fell and we looked down an almost sheer drop into Kentmere Reservoir directly below us. Treading very carefully, we continued along the path to the foot of a high crag. It was a final barrier between us and the summit of the Pass and we stopped to rest and check the ropes holding the packs.

'Pull the breast strap a bit tighter,' I called. 'We must make sure the pack-saddle doesn't slip back or we'll be in trouble.'

Philip adjusted the thick leather strap and with a gentle pull on Thor's lead rope, Abi led him round the boulders, up the narrow path that climbed the precipice in a series of zigzags. There was no opportunity to stare at the view as the path was very badly washed away in places and one slip would have sent Thor crashing down to the rocks below. We puffed and panted our way slowly towards the top and suddenly the climbing was over. Harter Fell towered above us on our right and stretching away to our left was a peak with the peculiar name of Mardale Ill Bell.

'What a relief,' gasped Abi, sinking down on a pile of rocks, 'I could do with a drink of water.'

'Me too,' said Philip, sucking in lungfuls of air. 'Can we have some now or do we have to wait until we reach the top of High Street?'

'Well, I've got a little surprise for you,' I said with a grin. 'I knew you'd be thirsty after this climb so I filled an extra water container. It's in my rucksack.'

'Oh great,' whooped Philip. 'I've got a packet of lemonade crystals somewhere.'

He filled our mugs, poured a bowl of water for Thor and Sammy, and we lay back against the boulders and sipped the cool lemonade. It tasted delicious. The sun was very hot and I had closed my eyes to rest them from the glare when a few spots of water landed on my face. Thinking it was either Abi or Philip playing a joke, I said, 'I shall get very cross with the person who is throwing water at me.'

'We're not throwing water at you,' said Philip, 'it's raining.'

'It's what?' I cried, leaping to my feet.

'It's raining,' repeated Philip. 'Look at that cloud.'

I could hardly believe my eyes. One minute the sun had been beating down from a clear sky and now a large black cloud had appeared from nowhere. Almost before we could pull on our waterproofs, the spots of rain increased to a frenzied downpour that had Thor snorting with fear and pulling madly at the rope tethering him to a rock. I quickly untied him and we pushed on up the ridge towards Mardale Ill Bell, almost blinded by the force of the rain, but there was not an atom of shelter anywhere. We staggered on and reached a cairn marking the top of Mardale Ill Bell when, miraculously, the rain stopped and the sun came out again.

'We have the silliest weather in the world,' grumbled Abi, removing her waterproofs and stuffing them into her rucksack. 'I wish it would make its mind up.'

'What I can't understand,' said Philip, squeezing water out of his shirt collar, 'is that last night the sky was a deep red and in my fishing book it says "red sky at night, angler's delight". There's nothing delightful about being soaking wet.'

'Well you can't expect it to work, silly,' scoffed Abi, 'you're a walker not an angler. Anyway, you've got it wrong, it's "shepherd's delight".'

'No it isn't,' argued Philip. 'I'll get the book out if you like and you can see for yourself.'

'Don't bother,' I interrupted, 'we must be on our

way, we've got High Street to climb yet. Abi, will you lead Thor please.'

The flat summit of High Street looked very close, but the distance was deceptive. A path which seemed to lead in the right direction soon disappeared into a bog and we were left to find our own way up a long ridge covered in thick tussock-grass. At first it was heavy going for Thor. He tripped over the hard tufts of grass and slid into the hollows of soft peat, but as we climbed higher the ground became firmer and levelled out. With a loud cheer, Abi and Philip raced each other to be first to touch the concrete pillar marking the summit of High Street. Though the sun was still shining bravely the blue sky had turned grey and a chilly breeze pulled at the tufts of sparse heather dotted across the summit plateau. We agreed that soup would be more welcome than a cold drink and, in the shelter of a wall, the stove was assembled and the aroma of Scotch broth wafted into the thin air.

'Isn't it a strange name to call a mountain,' said Abi, as we sat against the wall and dipped oatcakes into our mugs of soup. She had the map spread over her knees and was studying our route. 'High Street. I wonder who gave it that name.'

'The Romans,' I said, reaching for the pan of soup and topping up the mugs, 'and what's really fascinating is that where we are sitting now is part of the same path we used when we left Ravenglass and walked through Eskdale. It was a great Roman highway which started at Ravenglass and connected forts they built in Eskdale and Ambleside. This fell, with its long, flat ridge, stretches for about twenty miles, so you can imagine how useful it must have been when they were advancing north towards Scotland. High Street was the perfect name for it.'

High Street

'Gosh,' breathed Philip, his wild imagination working overtime. 'I can just see the Romans charging along here in chariots, waving their swords in the air and chopping the natives' heads off.'

'Oh, you are a fiendish little horror,' squealed Abi. 'Stop it, you're putting me off my soup. The Romans were nice people, they built baths and things and my teacher said that they invented ice cream.'

'Invented ice cream,' jeered Philip. 'How could anyone have invented ice cream? There's always been ice cream, even when grown-ups were at school!'

The sound of approaching voices put a stop to the argument and a party of cheerful hikers arrived and crowded around Thor to examine the pack-saddle and offer him pieces of chocolate.

'It must have been a great sight to watch the fell ponies racing up here in the old days,' shouted one of the hikers as they departed towards Kentmere. 'You ought to reintroduce it.'

I waved my acknowledgement as they disappeared over the ridge.

'Fell pony racing up here?' said Abi, looking puzzled, 'what is he talking about?'

'It was chariot racing,' said Philip gleefully, 'I knew I was right. The Romans used to race each other and the one that lost had to fight a lion.'

'What rubbish,' said Abi, shaking with laughter. 'Where does he get these wild ideas from? Didn't your teacher ever tell you it was the Christians that fought lions, not Romans.'

Philip looked crestfallen, but he soon bounced back. 'Oh well, I don't care. If it was Christians, I'll bet they weren't girl Christians.'

Abi had no answer to that and took a sudden interest in dismantling the stove.

'If you two would stop arguing for a minute,' I said, 'I'll tell you about fell pony racing. It had nothing to do with the Romans, in fact fell ponies were not bred until hundreds of years after the Romans had left Britain, but that's another story and there isn't time to talk about it now. It was local shepherds and farmers who started the pony racing. Nowadays, Lake District farmers take stray sheep back to each other's farms in vehicles, but in the old days farmers living in the valleys and dales round High Street used to meet once a year on the summit to hand back stray sheep they had collected during the year. It was a long walk just to exchange a few sheep so they made it a real day out. They organised sports, with competitions for wrestling, fell racing, hunting, singing and horn blowing. A lot of farmers rode up on fell ponies and one of the highlights of the day was a pony race from the summit cairn of High Street to Thornthwaite Crag. That's the peak you can see sticking up there at the southern end of the fell. They used to call it "Racecourse Hill".'

'But if they were galloping, how did they stop themselves falling over the edge?' asked Philip.

'It's a good point,' I said. 'Perhaps one or two did fall over when racing first started, because eventually they made a rule that if a pony went faster than a trot the rider would be disqualified. No doubt the farmers tried all sorts of ways to get their ponies to trot faster than their neighbours' and some people say it's one of the reasons why a good fell pony can trot faster than some horses can canter.'

'I'd love to see the ponies racing along here,' said Abi eagerly. 'Why don't they have races now?'

'Well I'm afraid that's life. Things go out of fashion and loose popularity as time goes by. Very few farms use fell ponies these days and since every farmer has a vehicle the annual meets are held in the valleys. The High Street pony races are part of history now.'

The sound of thunder in the distance warned that bad weather was not far away and, bundling the stove and pan into a bag, we beat a rapid retreat from High Street's exposed summit, down the north ridge to the Knott, an imposing little peak standing out from the main ridge like the battlements of a castle. It was an impressive view down a steep sided valley close to Hartsop, but there was little time to enjoy it. Thunder was rumbling ever closer and a few heavy spots of rain heralded worse to come. Sammy was frightened by the thunder and walked close behind me, whimpering each time it boomed round the fells. Thor took an excruciatingly long time to negotiate the path down the side of the Knott and though each clap of thunder sounded closer than the last, I dared not hurry him. The surface of the path was very badly eroded and each step had to be taken with the utmost care. At the foot of the Knott we were still a long way from Patterdale and we hurried along a boggy path towards Angle Tarn. The bog petered out at a long expanse of shattered rock which further delayed us while Thor was coaxed across awkward steps and round large boulders and all the time the storm drew nearer. Soon the glistening waters of Angle Tarn came into sight and, slithering down to it on a switchback of shiny peat, we reached the safety of a good path. Thor was panting with the exertion of being almost dragged along in an effort to keep ahead of the storm and when he spied the tarn he insisted on taking a long drink, pausing between mouthfuls to gaze imperturbably at the approaching clouds.

'Come on Thor, we'll be caught in the storm,' yelled Abi and Philip, but Thor simply licked his lips, sucked up another mouthful of water and gazed into space.

'You are a thickhead at times,' I bawled, grabbing his rope and leading him back on to the path. 'If we don't get off this fell soon, we'll be in trouble.'

We had only gone a short way when the storm burst over us. We were blasted and buffeted by the fierce squall, but to move faster than a snail's pace would have been exceedingly dangerous. Away from the safety of the broad plateau by the tarn, the path traversed airily across the side of the fell and we looked down an almost sheer drop into the valley. A short section of the path had been washed away by previous rainstorms and guiding Thor across it was a nightmare. The waterlogged ground broke away under his weight and for a heart-stopping second he almost toppled over the edge. With a huge leap he bounded across the gap and as he did so the ground where he had been standing slid away and poured down the fellside in an avalanche of boulders and mud.

'Gosh!' exclaimed Philip. 'That was a near thing. I wouldn't like to cross there again.'

Half hidden under her anorak hood, Abi looked as though she had seen a ghost. 'I was really frightened when Thor started to slide,' she said. 'I hope we don't have to cross any more places like this.'

'No, we're safe now,' I assured her. 'A short distance ahead of us is Boredale Hause and it's all downhill from there.'

Wave after wave of driving rain sluiced down on us, making progress very difficult, but when we reached Boredale Hause and the start of the pack-horse track to Patterdale, the worst was over. The buildings of Side Farm which from high above had looked so tiny, grew larger as we approached and though the rain did its best to make us feel miserable, it failed. We were so happy about reaching Patterdale, we sang all the way down to the farmhouse.

'You can't camp in this weather,' said Mike Taylforth, the farmer, as we dripped water on to his porch carpet. 'Carry on down the lane for about half a mile and you'll come to a barn. You'll be much drier in there.'

We found the barn in the corner of a field and, having rewarded Thor with chocolate biscuits and mint cake, we turned him loose to gorge himself on the thick grass. Inside the barn it was dark and smelt of musty hay, but there was plenty of room to move around and it was a great joy to change into dry clothes. An old farm trailer made an ideal table to prepare dinner and when I assembled the stove Abi made a meal of dried potatoes mixed with chunks of corned beef, followed by pâté and biscuits and the last of the fruit cake. During the night a strong wind moaned round the barn and drove the rain against the roof slates, but snug in our sleeping-bags on the trailer, we slept undisturbed, with Sammy stretched across us.

The sound of a cow bellowing in the field jolted me awake the following morning. It was almost dark in the barn, but when I looked at my watch I was amazed to

A change from camping

discover it was nearly nine thirty.

'Come on, it's time to get up,' I shouted. 'Are you awake?'

'Yes,' came the muffled reply from inside the sleeping-bags, but there was no movement.

'Find them, Sammy,' I ordered. Sammy wriggled into a sleeping-bag and began to lick the occupant. It was Abi.

'Go away, you horrible dog,' she complained, pulling the sleeping-bag over her head, 'I'm trying to sleep.'

But Sammy thought it was a marvellous game and dived on top of her.

'Ouch, get him off,' she yelled, 'I'll get up.'

Philip did not wait for Sammy's attentions, he kicked off his sleeping-bag and was dressed in a flash.

'Open the door and see what the weather is like,' I said. Lifting the heavy iron catch, he pushed the door open and immediately the barn was filled with brilliant sunlight.

'Come and look,' shouted Philip from outside, 'it's a super day.'

One of the nice things about the Lake District is that although it rains a lot, when the weather does clear up and the sun shines down out of a blue sky, it is an experience never to be forgotten. The barn was perched high on the fellside and we had an absolutely breathtaking view across Patterdale to the sharp peak of Dollywaggon Pike and the long, spiky ridge of Striding Edge, which leads to perhaps the most popular of all the Lakeland summits, Helvellyn, looking down from its lofty height of nine hundred and fifty metres. Below the barn, the surface of Ullswater flashed and sparkled in the bright sunlight and a red funnelled steamer sailed across the calm water, leaving a wide, rippling wake behind it. Where the field reached the edge of the lake, a heron was standing on a rock, glaring at a group of calves playing 'chase me Charlie' round a tree and spoiling his fishing by rushing into the water. In the end he gave up and, with wings flapping and spindly legs trailing, he took off and headed for a quiet bay on the opposite side of the lake. Thor was fast asleep under the shade of a tree, totally unaware that he was surrounded by a herd of inquisitive cows, who sniffed and snorted at the strange creature which had mysteriously arrived in their field. As they sniffed they became bolder and one cow mooed loudly in Thor's ear. He shot to his feet as if he had been stung and the terrified cows took one look at the huge, black beast rearing in front of them, then careered madly away, tails in the air and bawling with fright. They crowded through a gate at the far end of the field and were gone. Thor watched them go with a puzzled expression on his face then, with a long sigh, sank on to the grass again and continued his sleep.

'How would you like to spend tonight on top of Helvellyn?' I asked as we sat in the sun outside the barn and ate our breakfast.

'What a smashing idea,' exclaimed Abi. 'Would we camp up there?'

'No, there's a walled shelter on the top. It hasn't got a roof, but we'll take plenty of clothes and food and sit there and watch the sun come up.'

'Oh great,' said Philip. 'I've always wanted to see the dawn from the top of a mountain. Won't it be very cold without a tent and sleeping-bag though?'

'Well that depends a lot on the weather. It seems fairly settled now and provided we've enough warm clothes we will be safe enough. We'll have a rest day today and dry our wet clothes, then in the early evening we'll have a meal and set off for the summit.'

'Will we go along Striding Edge?' asked Philip

eagerly. 'I've heard it's a knife edge ridge with a fantastic drop on either side.'

'Well, it's not quite as bad as that,' I said, 'but it's certainly a narrow ridge and needs to be crossed very carefully. We'll go along it to the summit of Helvellyn and tomorrow we'll climb down Swirral Edge to Red Tarn and rejoin the Patterdale path. If you look at the map you'll see we'll be walking in roughly the shape of a horseshoe. It's only about eight miles altogether but there's a lot of climbing involved.'

Tying a rope between two trees, we hung our wet clothes over it and spent the rest of the morning lazing in the sun, cleaning our boots and coating the packsaddle with dubbin.

'It's to make it supple and waterproof,' said Philip, with the superior air of one who has spent hours rubbing it into his football boots. Abi pretended she did not hear him.

'By the way,' she said, vigorously polishing lengths of harness with a piece of cloth and handing them to me, 'when we were on High Street yesterday, you said you would tell us about fell ponies.'

'Oh yes,' said Philip. 'I'm going to write about fell ponies in my notebook. If the Romans didn't breed them, then where did they come from in the first place?' As he spoke, he dabbed his face with a cloth, forgetting he had just dipped it in the dubbin tin and instead of mopping up sweat he plastered his forehead with sticky brown dubbin. 'Bother,' he said irritably, trying hard not to say anything stronger, 'it's all over my face.'

Abi giggled uncontrollably. '"It makes it supple and waterproof,"' she mimicked. Philip glared at her and stalked off to the barn to find a dry cloth.

It was some time later, when we were sitting in the shade of a tree eating biscuits and cheese and drinking lemonade brought from the farm, that the subject of fell ponies came up again.

'The strange thing about the fell pony,' I said, 'is that although it is considered to be the native pony of the Lake District, it originally came from Galloway in southern Scotland and, in fact, there's many an old Lakeland farmer who still calls them "Fell Galloways". They used to roam in wild herds and very likely, as food became scarce, some strayed into the Lake District by crossing the Solway Firth when the tide was low. The farmers would catch them and use them for work around the farm. But the true fell pony breed that Thor belongs to all descend from a stallion found roaming about on a moor to the east of the Lake District, after Bonnie Prince Charlie's army retreated back to Scotland in 1745. When the stallion was found he was grazing on ling, that's a kind of heather, so they called him "Ling-cropper".'

'Was it fell ponies that the smugglers used?' asked Philip.

'Yes,' I said, 'smugglers used them a lot and if a smuggler happened to be a farmer, as they often were, he would use them for ploughing as well. The fields were too steep to use large horses, so they used to hitch four ponies to a wooden plough. We've passed quite a number of slate mines on our travels — when quarrying started in the Lake District, the only way slates could be brought down to the roads was by pack-pony and all the quarries had stables to keep their ponies in at night. They were used a lot in Northumberland, in coal mines, as well.'

'Oh no,' exclaimed Abi. 'Surely they didn't take them under the ground in mines. It's cruel.'

'Well it doesn't sound very nice, I admit, but the miners were very fond of their ponies and always made sure they were well fed. They even got a week's holiday each year, which is probably more than the miners got.'

'I still think it's cruel,' persisted Abi. 'Imagine lovely ponies like Thor being shut up in a dark mine and covered in dust, it's horrible.' The thought of it made her feel sorry for Thor and she ran over to where he was sleeping to give him a handful of biscuits. He was not quite sure what all the fuss was about, but he snatched the biscuits out of Abi's hand and ambled off down to the lake for a drink. Had he been able to talk, he might have explained that the closest he has ever been to the dark depths of a mine was the time he sneaked into a building, thinking it was my pony nut store, and it was only when the door slammed shut behind him, he found himself trapped all night in the coal-shed!

Chapter Seven

About five o'clock we had a light tea, packed our rucksacks with waterproofs, spare sweaters, socks, gloves and balaclava helmets, torches, first aid kit, map and compass, mint cake, chocolate and lemonade crystals. Leaving Thor in the field, we put Sammy on a lead and set off through Patterdale village to Grisedale and a rocky path climbing diagonally upwards towards the skyline and Striding Edge. There was a large party of lads and girls ahead of us, heavily laden with tents and rucksacks and they stopped so often for rests we soon caught up with them. They were a very cheery bunch from a Youth Club in Edinburgh and were on their way to camp for the night at the edge of Red Tarn. We promised to look out for them on the following morning and, with a wave and lots of shouts of 'enjoy yourselves', 'see you tomorrow', we left them having a friendly argument about whether the girls should help to carry the rucksacks.

When we left the barn the weather was very pleasant, the sun shone from an almost cloudless sky and every ridge and peak stood out in the clear air. But almost as soon as we set foot on the path to Striding Edge the weather began to change. Cloud began to drift in from the west, thin wisps of white at first, but as we climbed higher it increased to thick blobs of grey that settled on the summit of Helvellyn and poured down on

Patterdale Village with Helvellyn in the background (left skyline)

to Striding Edge like a cauldron of porridge boiling over. A chilly wind sprang up among the rocks making the bracken dance and ruffling the wool of the sheep scattered over the fellside. The sun took one look at the changing scene and retreated behind a cloud.

We toiled up the rough path until a large, flat rock provided an opportunity to rest and get our breath back. Philip lay with his chin on Sammy and stared upwards at the clouds drifting over the ridge.

'It seems to be getting thicker,' he said miserably. 'I hope we don't have to go back.'

'Isn't it just typical,' stormed Abi. 'It's been hot and sunny all day and as soon as we decide to do something exciting the silly weather has to spoil it.'

'Don't worry, it's not as bad as it looks,' I said, trying to sound cheerful. 'It might ruin the view, but it won't stop us sleeping on the top. We'll carry on until we reach Striding Edge and see what conditions are like up there.'

I hoped I sounded convincing. Although I did not show it, I was worried about the change in the weather and at the back of my mind I knew there was a distinct possibility that we might have to abandon the plan to sleep on the summit and retreat to the barn. Up and up we climbed, staggering over mounds of loose rubble and peat, where winter storms had torn away the surface of the path. Conversation was out of the question, every ounce of strength was needed to force our legs to keep moving towards Striding Edge, looming tantalizingly close above our heads. The path steepened and became even rougher, but with a burst of energy we clambered up on to the ridge and sank down behind a large rock. Philip's face was almost as red as his hair.

'I'm absolutely worn out,' he gasped, 'can we have a drink?'

'Not just yet,' I said, 'we'll save it till later.'

'But why?' howled Abi, 'I'm so thirsty I could drink a whole lake.'

'You're only thirsty because it was a hard slog up the path. If you have a drink now you'll hardly taste it and there's only about a pint between us. Later on we'll find a sheltered place away from this wind and stop for a drink and something to eat.'

The ridge leading to Striding Edge ran from east to west and started with easy walking along the top of Blaeberry Crag. The cloud, although it swirled and spiralled around the crags, was not as thick as it seemed from below and the summit of Helvellyn was clearly visible ahead of us. It was a tremendous boost to morale

Striding Edge on a clear day

and we surged forward through a huge heap of boulders to the top of High Spying How. Here the tearing action of the glaciers millions of years ago had piled the rocks up on edge and the easy walking was over. In front of us stretched a true mountain ridge, narrow jagged rock and a sheer drop on either side.

'It's fabulous,' exclaimed Philip, bracing himself against the wind. 'I've never seen anything like it.'

Abi was more down to earth. 'Is it safe?' she asked, looking dubiously at the thin path running along the crest and climbing a steep spur to the summit of Helvellyn.

'You've absolutely nothing to worry about,' I assured her. 'Striding Edge is one of the safest ridges in the Lake District in good weather. There's a little bit of rock scrambling at the end of it, but you'll manage all right.'

'What about Sammy?' said Philip.

'He'll probably manage better than us,' I said, 'but we must keep him in front of us all the time, in case he comes barging past and knocks us over the edge.'

The wind increased slightly and we slithered down to the shelter of a large rock to pull on our sweaters and waterproofs and eat a bar of chocolate. Wisps of cloud began to drift around the rocks and when I stood up and looked along the ridge I could hardly believe my eyes. In the few minutes we had spent sheltering the weather had completely changed again. Long banks of cloud had obscured the summit and were gradually creeping along Striding Edge.

'Let's get going,' I called. 'Keep close behind me and don't loose sight of each other.'

Helped along by the wind, the cloud soon enveloped us, but lifted again after a few minutes to reveal Red Tarn far below on our right. Again the cloud closed in, reducing visibility to a few metres and we were forced to stop. By now it was late in the evening and darkness was not far away. Soon I would have to make a decision to go on or go back. The cloud lifted once more and we made a little progress but when it returned it was so thick I could hardly see the two shadowy figures walking close behind me.

'It's no use,' I said. 'We can't go on in this, it's far too dangerous; we'll have to go back.'

'Oh no,' groaned Philip, 'we've come all this way and we're so close to the top. Can't we wait until the cloud lifts?'

'No,' I said firmly. 'I realize it's very disappointing for you, but it's better to be safe than sorry. We might have to wait a long time for the cloud to lift and it'll be dark soon.'

'Couldn't we sleep up here?' asked Abi. 'We could find a rock and shelter behind it.'

'Are you serious?' I said, half expecting her to admit she was only joking, but I was wrong.

'Yes, let's sleep here. I've always wanted to sleep on a mountain and I might not get the chance again.'

'Me too,' said Philip. 'I don't mind if it's cold.'

'Well all right,' I said, 'there's a wide ledge just in front of us. We'll be safe enough there and if the weather turned really nasty we could easily escape back along the ridge. Let's get settled before dark.'

The ledge was not far below the ridge and we clambered down to it and spread our rucksacks out to sit on. Wearing our sweaters, thick trousers and waterproofs, finished off with a scarf, gloves and woollen balaclava helmet, we were comfortably warm and Sammy lying across our legs made an excellent hot-water bottle. The ledge was about two and a half metres long by one metre wide and we shared it with a large iron monument bolted to a rock. It was in the shape of a gravestone and looked very creepy in the failing light, with long streamers of mist swirling round it like ghostly dancers. Abi leaned forward and shone her torch on the inscription.

Preparing for the night

'"In memory of Robert Dixon, Rodings, Patterdale,"' she read out, '"who was killed on this place on the 27th day of November 1858 when following Patterdale Foxhounds."'

'Following Patterdale Foxhounds?' echoed Philip. 'Surely he didn't ride a horse along here.'

'No, he wasn't on a horse,' I said. 'This sort of ground is too rough for horses. He would be following hounds on foot and very likely he slipped on the rock and fell over the edge. If it wasn't for the mist, you would be able to look down from our ledge, a very long way, almost vertically to the ground below.'

Abi shrank back and wriggled between Philip and me. 'Ugh,' she shivered, 'I'm glad I can't see over the edge.'

We lay back against the hard rock and listened to the sounds of the mountain night. On the ridge above us the wind moaned through the deep fissures in the rock, rising and falling like the sound of a giant organ. Ravens called to each other with their strange 'kronk, kronk' and swished invisibly over our ledge in a flurry of wings. The cry of a lamb searching for its mother drifted up from far below and, as the wind changed direction, it brought the sound of water from a distant beck as it poured down the fellside. Now and then, Helvellyn stirred in its sleep and sent stones rattling and crashing down the screes into Nethermost Cove. We dozed for an hour or two and about midnight a break appeared in the mist and revealed a full moon suspended in an inky sky. It closed in again quickly but the moon shining through the mist cast an eerie light over our ledge and as if at a magic signal, the cold, sterile ground around us became alive with beetles scurrying hither and thither and delicate white moths flitted across our feet. At first I thought I was dreaming, but Abi saw them too.

'What on earth can they find to live on at this height?' she said, brushing off a column of beetles advancing up her boots.

'I don't know,' I said. 'Perhaps the beetles find food in the heather and grass, but I can't imagine what attracts moths up here.'

Philip stirred and woke up. 'Oh, my leg's gone numb,' he groaned. 'Can we swop places so I can lie on my side?'

We moved round, but there was not enough room to stretch out. There were so many spiky rocks sticking out of the ground, no matter how many times we tossed and turned, finding a comfortable position was impossible. To pass the time we ate chocolate and played spelling games, but by two o'clock we were so tired we could hardly keep our eyes open.

'Am I hearing things, or is that thunder?' asked Philip, as we squirmed about in an effort to get off to sleep. We strained our ears and listened. Sure enough the sound of thunder rumbled round the fells in the distance, but it was a long way off. Half an hour later the rumblings were much closer, though it was difficult to tell which direction the storm was approaching from. A sharp crack of thunder to our right, in the direction of Dollywaggon Pike, reverberated round the corries like a roll of drums.

'It sounds as if it's getting closer,' said Abi nervously. 'Will we be all right here?'

'Yes, we're quite safe at the moment,' I said, 'but if it gets any nearer we may have to leave.'

The thunder broke again, not as loud this time and it appeared to be moving away. Another crack confirmed that the storm had retreated and I felt a lot happier.

Suddenly, a tremendous flash of lightning pierced the mist, followed by an ear-splitting crack of thunder right above us. The air hummed and crackled with electricity and almost immediately another flash lit up the rocks with a fantastic blue light and the most awful crack of thunder shook our ledge like an earthquake. Poor Sammy howled with fright and dived underneath my coat.

'Follow me, quickly,' I said urgently. 'We must get away from this iron monument in case it's struck by lightning.'

For some strange reason the mist suddenly lifted and, as I climbed on to the rock above the ledge I witnessed a most awesome sight. A tremendous fork of lightning struck a pinnacle at the end of Striding Edge and bounced along the ridge, sparking like an electric cable. The entire area was lit by an incredibly powerful light, but within seconds it had gone and the ridge was plunged into darkness. Slowly the mist settled again, the crackle of electricity ceased and the rumbles of thunder receded into the distance. The storm had passed over. A few chunks of rock, broken off by the lightning, bounced down the fellside into the soft ground below and all was quiet.

'Are you all right?' I called down to Abi and Philip.

'Yes, we're fine, but it was scary while it lasted,' came the reply.

I rejoined them on the ledge and we managed to sleep for an hour or so before the dark mist slowly turned white with the approaching dawn. Visibility was still down to a few metres and it was bitterly cold.

'I'm absolutely frozen,' said Abi, thrashing her arms about. 'What time is it?'

'Nearly five o'clock,' I said, looking at my watch. 'Give Philip a shake and we'll do some exercises to warm you up.'

Philip grunted and tottered to his feet. 'Ggggosh,' he stuttered through chattering teeth, 'if it's so ccccold up here, I wonder what it's like on Everest.'

'You'll soon get warm,' I said. 'Climb up on the ridge.' To have met three hooded figures and a dog, jogging backwards and forwards along a part of Striding Edge would have given the strongest nerves a dreadful shock, but fortunately we had the ridge to ourselves and after twenty minutes we had warmed up and were ready for breakfast. It was only a bar of chocolate and a piece of mint cake each, washed down with cold water mixed with lemon crystals but it was very welcome.

'Wouldn't it be nice if we could see the view,' said Philip, licking sugary lemon crystals out of his mug. 'I wish this mist would go away.'

'There's no chance of that unless the sun comes out,' I said, 'and even then it could be late morning before it has any effect.'

'What are we going to do then?' asked Abi. 'Go back the way we came?'

'Not necessarily,' I said. 'Apart from the mist, the weather is quite good and if you are both feeling up to it, we'll go to the top of Helvellyn.

'Oh great,' they chorused, 'let's go on.'

'All right, it's the same rules as yesterday: keep close together and don't lose sight of each other.'

Sammy bounded on ahead into the mist and we followed, picking our way carefully along the narrow crest of Striding Edge. Even though the mist obscured the view beyond a few metres, we were very conscious of the drop on both sides and moved with the utmost care. For the most part, it was fairly easy, but right at the end of Striding Edge, barring our way to the summit, was a rock chimney about fifteen metres deep. In clear weather it would present little difficulty for anyone not afraid of a short rock climb, but when we peered over the edge the swirling mist made it hard to see the holds. I helped Sammy down first and left him guarding my rucksack while I went back to guide Abi and Philip, but they swarmed down without any hesitation. A short steep path led upwards and almost before we realized it we were standing on the summit of Helvellyn in front of a large cairn of stones.

'It's another monument,' cried Abi, using the sleeve of her anorak to wipe the moisture off a plaque fixed to the cairn. 'It's something about a dog guarding a skeleton. Come and look.'

The inscription was difficult to make out in the poor light and Philip shone the torch on it to read it aloud.

'"Beneath this spot were found in 1805 the remains of Charles Gough, killed by a fall from the rocks. His dog was still guarding the skeleton."'

'Isn't that sad,' said Abi softly. 'I wonder what happened.'

'It's a well known story, but no one is quite sure what happened,' I said. 'According to local people, Charles Gough was from Manchester and often spent his holidays in Patterdale, fishing and walking the fells with his little terrier called "Foxy". The year he died he stayed in Patterdale for a few days and then set off to walk over Striding Edge and Helvellyn to stay at an inn at Wythburn, on the edge of Thirlmere. He climbed the path to Striding Edge, carrying a pack and his fishing-rod, with little Foxy trotting beside him, and he was never seen again. There were no telephones in those days and the landlord of the inn where he had been staying naturally thought that since he hadn't returned he must have reached Thirlmere. No one gave him a thought until about three months later a shepherd gathering sheep at Red Tarn heard a dog barking among the rocks below Helvellyn. When he went to investigate he discovered a skeleton and Foxy standing guard over it. Apparently Gough had got lost in bad weather and fallen down the crags. The little dog couldn't understand that Gough was dead and, for three months, she had stayed by his side barking as loudly as she could in the hope that someone would bring help. When the shepherd found her she was so weak she could hardly walk, so he wrapped her in his coat and took her home with him and looked after her until she went to live with one of Charles Gough's relations.'

'What a lovely story,' said Philip. 'If I'm ever allowed to have a dog I'm going to call it "Foxy".'

Abi was staring at the inscription on the plaque as

though she was trying to read it through again, but as she turned, her face was caught in the light of Philip's torch and she hurriedly brushed aside a flood of tears.

'Come on, you great softy,' I said, squeezing her arm gently, 'let's go, it's getting cold.'

Visibility on the summit was down to a metre or so and I worked out a compass course to take us first to the Ordnance Survey's concrete pillar marking the highest point at nine hundred and fifty metres, then to Swirral Edge and the start of our descent to Red Tarn. At first Swirral Edge was rather like Striding Edge in reverse and in the mist it required great care. Stone shoots that looked like paths often ended on the edge of an abyss and a lot of time was spent making sure we were heading in the right direction. Unlike Striding Edge, which is part of a long ridge, Swirral Edge slants down and, having safely negotiated an awkward, rocky section we followed a good path to level ground. We could hear voices calling to each other through the mist and by the edge of Red Tarn we almost walked into the tents belonging to the Edinburgh party we had met on the way up the day before. The leader said the girls in the party had been terrified by the thunder and had spent most of the night weeping.

'This wee lassie must be very brave to have spent the night on Helvellyn in that sort of weather,' he said, smiling at Abi.

'There'll be no living with her now,' teased Philip as we left the campers and set off again, 'she'll be so big-headed because someone said she is brave, I'll have to ask permission to speak to her.'

'It proves that girls are just as good at things as boys,' said Abi, pretending to be haughty. 'You may carry my rucksack if you wish, my man.'

Philip replied by blowing a large raspberry.

I set a compass course from Red Tarn and after floundering through a wilderness of waterlogged peat, we reached a stile over a wall and rejoined the path leading to Patterdale. To our great joy we walked out of the mist and looked down on a sunlit valley and green fields.

'Are you tired?' I asked, as we stopped to pull off our waterproofs and spare sweaters.

'Yes, a little bit,' said Abi.

'My eyelids feel like lead,' said Philip. 'I could sleep for a week.'

'Well, I must say I am very proud of you both,' I said, 'and when we reach the village I'm going to buy you a slap up breakfast and then we'll go back to the barn and you can sleep for as long as you like.'

The only café in Patterdale spoilt my promise of breakfast by being closed and, very disappointed, we made our way back to the barn and lay in our sleeping bags with mugs of hot Oxo. Lulled by the warm drink and cosy sleeping-bags, we drifted off into a deep sleep. It was well into the afternoon before we surfaced and outside the barn the sun was beating down from a cloudless sky.

'Isn't it infuriating? Look at Helvellyn now!' exclaimed Abi, pointing at the ridge. 'There isn't a cloud to be seen.'

Every pinnacle stood out mockingly against the pale blue background of the sky and the air was so clear we could easily make out the concrete pillar on the summit.

'That's the way it is with the fells,' I said; 'the weather can be very unpredictable at times and you just have to learn to live with it. Mind you,' I added, jokingly, 'if you want to spend another night on Helvellyn and watch the sun rise, we can set off after tea!'

'No thank you,' said Abi quickly. 'I think I would

prefer to sleep in the barn if it's all right with you.'

'I wouldn't mind,' said Philip boldly, 'but I'm too tired to go tonight. I'll go tomorrow though.'

'Don't take me seriously,' I laughed. 'I'm only ribbing you. I'm sure it will be a long time before you forget the night on Striding Edge.'

We took a picnic down to the edge of the lake and spent the rest of the afternoon lazing in the sunshine and throwing sticks into the water for Sammy to retrieve.

'I think I'll fish for a while,' said Philip staring thoughtfully at the water. 'There's a tree hanging over the water up there and my fishing book says it's the sort of place where trout lie.'

He ran back to the barn and returned with his fishing-rod and a cardboard box full of worms he had dug out from under the stones in the field. Very solemnly he assembled his rod and went through the ritual of throwing pieces of bread into the water before he carefully placed a worm on the hook and, with a great flourish, cast it into the lake.

'I wish I was a good swimmer,' said Abi, grinning mischievously. 'I'd love to swim underwater and tie an old boot on the end of his line.'

'It would be great fun,' I laughed, 'but you know how lucky he is. Someone would probably come along and discover the boot was an interesting relic and swop him a bag of fish for it!'

Despite his enthusiasm, Philip never seemed to have much success with his fishing. The weather would be too cold, or too hot; the water too deep, or too shallow; the sun too bright, or not bright enough and, of course, there were always people. Though he often searched frantically through his fisherman's bible, there was no advice to be found on what to do about people and the shore of Ullswater was seething with them. No sooner had he cast his line than a large party, with yapping dogs and noisy children, arrived and proceeded to throw stones into the water and shriek with laughter when the dogs jumped in after them. While mums and dads lay on the grass, listening to a portable radio, the children paddled an inflatable dinghy round the bay, hotly pursued by their friends, trying to tip them out of it. They were having a marvellous time, but the noise frightened away every fish for miles. Philip abandoned his fishing spot to the revellers and, carrying his rod over his shoulder, walked dejectedly along the lake shore.

'It's a pity there aren't any sharks in Ullswater,' he muttered fiercely, as he trudged by on his way to the barn.

We had eaten very little in the previous twenty-four hours and for our evening meal we gorged ourselves on sausages, beefburgers and new potatoes from the farm, followed by biscuits, cheese and fresh fruit. It was a lovely evening and, after we had eaten, we sat outside against the barn wall and gazed at the wonderful panorama of fells and woods. The picnickers, bathers and noisy outboard motors were gone from the lake and placid cows stood knee deep in the cool water, lifting their heads now and then to stare at a fleet of dinghies with brightly coloured sails, as they glided by. The lake steamer curved in a wide arc round the bay, its green hull and bright red funnel glistening in the setting sun, as the captain steered it gently towards Glenridding. With a final puff of smoke from the funnel, it eased against the pier and stopped. Another day was over.

'Where are we going tomorrow?' asked Philip, when we were in our sleeping-bags on the trailer.

'Well, if you're not too worn out, I'd rather like to reach Borrowdale, if possible,' I replied. 'We'll walk up Grisedale, that's the valley where the Striding Edge path starts, climb up to Grisedale Tarn, then drop down to Grasmere. The village will be swarming with visitors at this time of the year and we could waste a lot of time looking for somewhere to camp. It's another six or seven miles to Borrowdale and there is a steep pass to climb over, but it will be worth it.'

'Let's go to Borrowdale,' said Abi drowsily.

'What about you Philip?' I said. There was no answer, he was fast asleep.

Chapter Eight

It took ages to find Thor the next morning. During our stay he had made friends with the cows and each day they took him on a tour of the fields and showed him their favourite hiding-places in the woods. We eventually found him snoozing contentedly under an old oak tree, surrounded by his tail-swishing, cud-chewing companions, who glared at us with watery red eyes and backed off, snorting angrily, when I slipped a halter over Thor's head and led him away to the barn. It was a perfect day for walking. Low cloud obscured the fell tops, keeping the hot sun at bay and it was pleasantly warm when we left Side Farm and followed a road round Patterdale Church to a broad track leading to Grisedale. On both sides of the narrow valley the fells towered into the clouds and when we reached the end of the level track and saw the old pack-horse route snaking upwards to a break in the clouds, it created an exciting feeling of venturing into the unknown. At first the uphill path was fairly easy, but crossing a wooden bridge over the raging waters of Grisedale Beck, it rose steeply to Ruthwaite Lodge, a climbers' hut perched on the side of the fell. It was a strenuous climb and by the time we reached the lodge our shirts were soaked in sweat and Abi's face was the colour of a beetroot.

'I'm aching all over,' she gasped, collapsing on the grass. 'I must have a rest.'

The pack-horse route in Grisedale with the Helvellyn range in the background

Philip lay on his stomach by the edge of a beck and sucked noisily at the water. 'That feels better,' he said, wiping his mouth with his shirt sleeve. 'I hope the rest of the path isn't as steep as this, I'm worn out already.'

The climb was nothing to Sammy and, as fresh as a daisy and lively as ever, he bounded up the hill with a stick in his mouth and dropped it on Abi.

'Oh go away, Sammy,' she groaned. 'I need my energy for walking, not for throwing sticks. Go and see Philip.'

But Philip pretended to be asleep. The trio of lazy humans stretched out on the ground was too much for Sammy and, with an impatient bark, he grabbed his stick and with his tail in the air, he trotted off up the path.

'Come on,' I called, 'if we don't catch up with the little pest he'll be in Grasmere hours before us.'

Beyond Ruthwaite Lodge the path became progressively rockier and, in places, was so rough and broken that Thor had to be led through it with great care. As we climbed higher the cloud began to break up and a hot sun beat down, lathering us in such a sweat that our already slow pace was reduced to a crawl.

'Not far now,' I shouted encouragingly. 'One more steep section and we'll reach Grisedale Tarn at the top of the Pass.'

We plodded relentlessly on up rock and scree until, to our immense relief, the path levelled out and there before us was Grisedale Tarn, nestling in a hollow between Dollywaggon Pike and Fairfield. Above the tarn, the path traversed across a wet, boggy hillside, then went to the opposite extreme, vanishing among a maze of broken rocks and scree. It was very difficult ground for Thor to negotiate carrying the heavy packs

Grisedale Tarn

and it required a lot of coaxing, and sometimes actually lifting his legs carefully over a particularly nasty obstacle, before we reached the edge of Grisedale Hause and looked down a long, narrow valley towards Grasmere. But the worst was by no means over. To reach the valley we were faced with a very steep descent down a tumbled mass of boulders and loose scree, gouged and twisted by countless winter storms.

'Should we tighten Thor's breeching?' asked Philip, as we sat on a slab of rock and worked out the safest line to take down the fell.

'Yes,' I replied, 'take it in as far as it will go, otherwise the saddle might slip forward.'

The adjustments completed, we worked our way down through the boulders in a series of long zigzags. It took a very long time and there were a few anxious moments when Thor skidded on the loose scree and almost fell over, but eventually we reached the bottom and followed a good path down the valley to the main Grasmere to Keswick road. It was extremely hot and we rested for a few minutes in the shade of a row of cottages.

'We've got a choice now,' I said, consulting the map. 'We can either go across the road and follow a lane which will bring us out on the path to Borrowdale, or we can walk down the main road to Grasmere to buy ice cream and join the Borrowdale path later.' There was no hesitation.

'Ice cream, please,' cried two hoarse voices and Sammy wagged his tail.

Grasmere village was crowded with tourists and our strange procession attracted a lot of attention as we tramped along the road. Cars pulled on to the verge while the occupants stared curiously out of the windows or shrank back in their seats when Thor bared his teeth at them. Actually he was only pulling faces whilst chewing a lump of mint cake, but the display of teeth was quite spectacular. A small crowd watched our every move and when we stopped in the main square to sit on a bench and share our ice cream with Thor and Sammy, cameras clicked away by the dozen. Abi blushed a deep scarlet when an elderly American, festooned with cameras, stopped in front of us and said to his wife, 'Gee, ain't this little blond haired girl cute. Hold it right there honey, I wanna shot of you feeding your horse with ice cream.'

A shout from the opposite side of the square drew the attention of the crowd around us and they hurried away towards a procession advancing down the road.

'Thanks a million, honey,' called the American to Abi. 'We gotta go and take a few shots of the rush-bearing now.' Ramming a new magazine of film into his cine camera, he dashed away and was soon lost in the crowd.

'What's rush-bearing?' asked Philip, standing on the seat and craning his neck to get a better view of the procession.

'I'll tell you as we go along,' I said, untying Thor's lead rope. 'If we don't leave now we might be hemmed in the square for hours.'

Following the direction of a signpost pointing to Easedale we set off up a narrow road just as the head of the procession of little girls carrying bunches of flowers entered the square.

'I'm sorry we couldn't stop to watch,' I said, as we tramped along the road, 'but if Thor had taken fright, goodness knows what might have happened. I wondered why there were such a lot of people in the village, it's the annual rush-bearing ceremony in Grasmere Church. It goes back to the time when country churches had earth floors and the villagers used to gather rushes to spread over the soil. Every year, about now, they cleared the church out and filled it with new rushes then everyone got together and had a party.'

'Has Grasmere Church still got an earth floor?' asked Abi, unable to believe that anyone could be so primitive.

'No, they have nice stone slabs to walk on, nowadays, and it's become more of a flower festival; that's why the girls we saw in the procession were carrying flowers instead of rushes.'

'I don't think we have a rush-bearing ceremony in Ennerdale,' said Philip. 'At least I've never heard of one.'

'They probably had one years ago,' I said, 'but it's more or less died out now in Cumbria. The only other one I know of is held at Ambleside, but I believe there are two or three other churches around that keep the tradition going.'

The surfaced road wound upwards above the village to a cluster of large houses, half hidden among the trees, then ended abruptly at the start of a pack-horse track. In the days before proper roads were built to connect the Lake District communities, the track must have been a very important link between Grasmere and Borrowdale. For some distance beyond the road end it was well surfaced with cobbles and flanked on either side by dry stone walls. After the rough and tumble of the journey from Patterdale, it was a joy to walk on a good track and we strode along at a cracking pace, keeping time with the clinking sound of Thor's iron shoes striking the hard ground.

'I'm ravenous,' announced Abi after we had been walking for half an hour or so. 'Can we stop and have something to eat?'

'That's a good idea, my stomach keeps rumbling,' said Philip. 'I could just eat a bowl of soup.'

'Well all right then,' I said, 'we'll stop soon and light the stove.'

A walled paddock by the bubbling waters of Easedale Gill provided grazing for Thor and an ideal place to assemble the stove and prepare a pan of soup. I was about to pour it into the mugs when Philip discovered that the mound of springy grass he was sitting on was an ants' nest. With a yell, he leaped to his feet and performed a lively war dance in an effort to shake off a horde of angry ants swarming up his legs. Round and round he went, almost kicking the stove over, but I managed to grab the pan of soup and run with it to safer ground. Abi lay on the grass, helpless with laughter, while poor Philip raced round the paddock jumping boulders and crashing through bracken.

'I've never seen him move so fast,' she gasped, tears of laughter running down her face. 'We ought to enter him for the Grand National.'

Apart from a few red blotches round his ankles, he was none the worse for the ant attack and dangling his feet in the beck for a few minutes helped to relieve the soreness.

'Isn't it strange that there aren't many farms in this valley,' Abi remarked when we had finished our soup and were sitting against a wall gazing at the view. 'Look at all these little fields, they must have belonged to farms at some time.'

'They still do,' I said. 'Every bit of land is owned by somebody, even the tops of the fells. In the old days those fields would be owned by several small farms, but as time went by it became harder to make a living and gradually the people moved away and the houses crumbled. Imagine having potatoes and bread for almost every meal with, perhaps, a piece of mutton now and then. They had milk from their own cows and made butter and baked bread, but the farmers' families never knew what it was like to eat the sort of food we have. Quite a number of families almost starved to death in the winter; in fact there's a very sad story told about a farmer who lived in this valley.

One winter's day, the farmer and his wife left their six children at home and walked over to Langdale to a farm sale. While they were there it began to snow heavily and everyone made for home. The farmer's friends wanted him and his wife to stay the night in Langdale but he was worried about the children left in the care of the eldest girl, who was only nine. Anyway, they wouldn't stop and were last seen climbing up the fell in the teeth of a gale. In Easedale, huge snowdrifts were building up around the farm and, though the children waited and waited, darkness came and they were so tired they all fell asleep. During the night the blizzard increased and by morning the children were completely snowed in and couldn't go for help. Little Agnes, the one who was nine, managed to milk the cow and give her brothers and sisters a drink, then they all huddled round the peat fire to keep warm. They were there for four days, living on very little food, before the blizzard died down and Agnes was able to stagger through the snowdrifts to the next farm for help. A search party was formed and they hunted for almost a week without success, but then dogs were brought in and they found the bodies of the farmer and his wife buried in the snow.'

'Isn't that awful,' sniffed Abi, wiping her eyes. 'I think I'm going to cry.'

'What happened to the children?' asked Philip, almost in a whisper.

'Most of them were adopted by local families and

William Wordsworth, the poet, who lived in Grasmere at the time, organized a relief fund for them and raised about five hundred pounds, quite a lot of money in those days. Even the Royal Family heard about the disaster and sent the children some money.'

A jovial party of hikers helped to dispel the gloom of the story of the Easedale children with their laughing and singing, as they strode down the path towards us. They crowded round Thor and Sammy, taking photographs and questioning us about our journey. What did we carry on our pack-saddle? Where did we sleep at night? Did we carry food for Thor and Sammy? And so on until our heads were in a whirl.

'Come on lads, we'll miss the bus,' shouted the party leader. 'We've half an hour to get to Grasmere.'

Immediately there was a stampede of bodies, swaying rucksacks and tartan socks, as they raced each other down the track. With a loud cheer they disappeared from view and, loading the bags on to Thor, we continued on our way.

Towards the head of the valley the track crossed a ford over Easedale Gill and followed a meandering course towards the skyline.

'Look at that lovely yellow flower,' called Abi, pointing to a long stemmed plant as we picked our way through a patch of bog. 'Let's find out what it is.'

Philip produced the flower book from his rucksack and we leafed through it.

'I think it's bog asphodel,' he said, pointing at a page of yellow flowers.

'Well, it could be,' said Abi, peering over his shoulder, 'but I'm not sure. I'll have another look at it.' She turned to the flower and stopped, with a puzzled expression on her face. 'Hey, it's gone!' she called.

'Gone? How could it have gone?' snorted Philip.

'Well it has, look for yourself.' All that remained was a short piece of stem poking out of the grass. We stared in amazement, wondering where the flower could have vanished to.

'I know what's happened,' said Abi slowly, 'Thor's eaten it.'

I opened his mouth and there, all chewed up, was the flower.

'You are a greedy brute, Thor,' I scolded, 'now we'll never know what it was.'

We hunted round the bog, but there was not another flower to be seen. Higher up the fell we identified bilberry and sphagnum moss, but it seemed that Thor had devoured the only specimen of the yellow flower in the whole valley.

At the head of the valley the track wound up through a mixture of bog and peat to Greenup Edge, a long ridge marking the boundary between Easedale and Stonethwaite in Borrowdale. It was a strenuous climb and, with sighs of relief, we flopped in the short grass at the top and quenched our thirst with lemonade crystals stirred into mugs of cool water. In Easedale the weather had been warm and sunny, but as we descended into Stonethwaite it changed abruptly. A cool breeze swished through the grass on the fellside and to the west, long bands of dark cloud were drifting in rapidly from the Irish Sea

'I hope it doesn't rain and spoil this lovely day,' said Abi looking anxiously at the sky.

Philip spat on his finger and held it up to judge the direction of the wind.

'My fishing book says that if the wind blows from the west during the summer the weather will be cloudy, with rain or showers, and the wind is blowing from the west now.'

'Oh that fishing book again!' said Abi, with a disdainful sniff. 'It thinks it knows everything. If it's as good at forecasting weather as it is about telling you where to catch fish, we'll probably have a heat wave.'

Philip did not have a chance to reply. We were crossing an expanse of wet ground when Thor suddenly sank up to his belly in a bog.

'Grab his lead rope and hold him,' I shouted. 'I'll untie the packs.'

But before I could reach the ropes Thor floundered forward and got himself well and truly stuck. The more he struggled the deeper he sank, until I was worried that he would disappear completely. Abi and Philip hung on grimly to the lead rope, while I talked to Thor and fumbled with the ropes holding the packs. When I worked my way round him I discovered he had fallen into an isolated bog hole and in front of him was firm ground.

'Pull hard,' I yelled and at the same time pushed with all my strength on his hindquarters. His front legs found a hold and, with a gurgle like water running down a drain, he heaved himself forward, spraying us with lumps of wet moss as he jumped to safety. Fell ponies are particularly courageous in awkward situations and, although it had been a nasty experience for him, Thor spotted a patch of juicy grass and was soon chewing as if nothing had happened. Abi and Philip rubbed the wet moss off his body with handfuls of heather and, with a quick check to see that his shoes had not been pulled off in the bog, I led him down the steep path towards Stonethwaite.

A man repairing a gap in a dry-stone wall watched us intently as we approached and I was delighted to find it was a friend of mine called John Bulman, who works for the Lake District National Park. As an

Upland Management Officer, John's job takes him and his men all over the Lake District, making sure that paths and gates are in good order, looking after fences and woodland and perhaps most important of all, helping visitors to understand the life of the Lake District. Like so many men born and bred into hill farming, he is an expert at building dry-stone walls and we stopped to watch him work.

'If you don't use cement, how do you stop the wall falling down?' asked Philip.

John balanced a large stone on top of two smaller ones, then stood back to check his work. 'It would use up all the cement in the country if every wall in the Lake District was built with it,' he laughed. 'In the old days farmers had to make do with what they could find on the fell. Come over here and I'll show you how it's done.'

'Can girls build walls?' asked Abi, anxious not to be left out.

'Aye lass, of course they can,' smiled John. 'Though it's the wrong job if you want to keep your hands soft and clean. The rough stone will make your skin feel like sandpaper.'

I put the hobbles on Thor to prevent him straying and, dumping their rucksacks and anoraks on the heather, Abi and Philip joined John at the wall.

'Well, the first thing you've got to learn about a dry-stone wall,' he said, 'is that, unlike the wall of a house, which stands upright, the sides of these walls, lean in towards the middle. If you look along this wall now, you'll see that it's wide at the bottom and narrow at the top and that's one of the reasons why it doesn't fall down.'

Philip craned his neck and sighted along the wall. 'I can see what you mean now,' he said, 'but how do you lay the big stones on the bottom, in the first place?'

'Well that's where the art of walling starts,' answered John. 'Usually the base of a wall is about a metre wide and we dig a trench about fifteen centimetres deep and lay the biggest stones in first. These are called footing stones and we lay them in two lines on either side of the trench and fill the gap with small stones.' He pointed to the gap in the wall. 'Look at this wall where it's fallen down and you'll see how it was started. When the footing stones are nicely bedded in then we start to build the wall. A builder using bricks to build a house lays a row of bricks first, then the next layer staggered, so that each brick lies across the joint of the ones below. We do the same, except that our stones are all shapes and sizes and you need to be able to judge which ones will fit together. As each row of stones is laid, the gap in the centre is filled up with small stones, or "hearting" if

Dry-stone walling

you want its proper name, so that the finished wall is solid. When a few rows have been laid, making sure each side of the wall is leaning in at an angle, then we put a line of "through" stones on. These are long stones the width of the wall and they help to keep the two sides together.' John bent down and put a few stones into place.

'Right Abi, you fill the middle with small stones and Philip can help me to put this through stone on.'

Philip panted with the exertion of lifting a heavy, flat stone and almost dropped it as he and John heaved it into place. We spent a very enjoyable time helping to repair the wall and Abi and Philip were very proud of the finished job.

'Couldn't have done better myself,' said John, examining a neat row of flat stones leaning at the same angle along the top of the wall. 'These are called "cam" stones by the way, and they are not put on just to make it look attractive, they stop sheep from jumping over the wall.' Pausing to look at his watch, he wiped his hands on the grass and pulled on his coat. 'Thanks for your help, you've worked hard. I'm off home now.'

Before he left I scribbled a message on a piece of paper and handed it to him. He read it slowly, then a broad grin spread across his face.

'Righto, I'll see to it,' he said, thrusting the note into his pocket.

Collecting Thor and whistling Sammy, who was busy hunting rabbits, we waved good-bye to John and continued down the fell.

'I'm exhausted,' puffed Abi. 'I can't wait to crawl into my sleeping-bag. Now I understand why farmers are so angry when people climb over walls and knock them down.'

'I'm going to write about wall building in my book,'

said Philip. 'It must have taken ages to build some of them. Look at that one over there, the through stones are enormous.'

Working with John had sparked off a new interest and instead of being simply a heap of stones, the walls were now an exciting part of the scenery. All the way to our campsite the walls around the fields were closely inspected and different building techniques discussed with an air of authority.

'Your walls look as if they might be "bellying out",' said Philip helpfully when the farmer came to our tent for his camping fee, later that evening.

He glared at Philip for a moment then turned on his heel. 'Cheeky young pup,' he muttered.

Chapter Nine

The clouds sweeping in from the west when we crossed the fell from Easedale had completely filled the sky by morning and when I peeped through the tent door it was dull and overcast and a chilly wind whined through the branches of the trees and cracked the nylon flysheet like a whip. The air was too cold to sit outside and we ate breakfast lying in our sleeping-bags. Hardly a word was spoken and an unusual atmosphere of gloom hung over us. It had nothing to do with the change in the weather.

'It's our last day, today, isn't it?' said Abi miserably.

'Yes, I'm afraid so,' I replied. 'Ennerdale is only a few hours' walk from here and we should reach it by this evening. It's hard to believe we've been away for nearly two weeks.'

'I could carry on for ever,' said Philip wistfully. 'I like exploring the fells and there must be places we haven't visited that are teeming with fish. If we could stay for another week I'm sure I could catch a trout or a pike or something.'

'You've certainly not had much luck with your fishing-rod, but cheer up, I've got a surprise for you. That note I gave to John Bulman yesterday, asked him to arrange with Jim Loxham, a local mountain guide, to take you rock climbing this morning.'

'Rock climbing!' cried Abi, almost bursting with

excitement. 'Oh that's marvellous, I've always wanted to go rock climbing.'

'Me too,' said Philip eagerly. 'Which crag are we going to climb on?'

I unfolded the map and spread it across the sleeping-bags. 'We are here, in Borrowdale, and to reach Ennerdale we have to climb up Honister Pass. There are dozens of small crags up there and I've asked Jim to meet us at ten o'clock by the Youth Hostel at the top of the Pass. We've got about two hours so let's leave as soon as we can.'

The bags were packed and the tent rolled up in record time and in less than half an hour we were toiling up Honister Pass. Above the tiny hamlet of Seatoller the tarmac road was very steep and a sudden shower of rain made the smooth surface treacherously slippery. Several times Thor stumbled and almost went down, but after a mile or so the road lost its steepness and, following a line of tourist cars, we zigzagged slowly upwards to the Youth Hostel perched on the summit. Jim was waiting for us and led the way up the fell to the foot of a crag. Thor was turned loose with the hobbles on and Sammy and I sat on a boulder and watched Jim preparing his equipment. Abi and Philip were each given a safety helmet and a special type of body harness made of strong webbing and they were ready to start.

'Any fool can climb a rock face,' Jim explained, 'but to climb it safely there are a few rules you have to learn. To be safe, you have to be comfortable so never reach too high and don't lift your feet higher than knee level. Also, never move a hand and a foot at the same time, always keep both feet and one hand on the rock while you reach up with the other hand, or keep two hands and one foot on the rock while you step up with the other foot.'

Preparing for the climb

They both doubled up with laughter when Jim demonstrated the wrong way to climb and fell off into the heather.

'Now look at the rock face we're going to climb,' said Jim. 'D'you see that ledge about ten metres up. Imagine we were roped together and I was standing on the ledge where Philip was climbing and he fell off, what would happen?'

'He would pull you off the ledge,' said Abi quickly.

'Exactly,' said Jim. 'So we have to have a way of safeguarding each other while we're climbing. It's called a belay and it's simply a means of tying yourself to the rock face when you are not actually climbing. The easiest way of belaying is with a sling like this.'

He produced a loop of rope and a large, steel clip. 'The sling is looped over a spike of rock and joined to your safety harness with this steel clip called a Karabiner and then if the person climbing slips, it should be possible to hold him on the rope without being pulled off yourself. Are you ready to have a go?'

They both nodded earnestly.

'Right then Philip, pay out the rope as I'm climbing.'

Jim moved steadily up the rock to the ledge and belayed. He hauled in the slack rope until it pulled taut.

'That's me,' Philip shouted.

'Climb when you're ready,' called Jim.

Philip stepped nervously on to the first foothold. 'Climbing,' he shouted.

'O.K.,' came the reply.

Philip's knees trembled as his hand searched feverishly for a hold.

'There's a hold just by your right shoulder,' called Abi. 'Yes, that's the one.'

He gasped with relief when his hand found it and, in a series of jerky movements, assisted by Jim pulling gently on the rope, he flopped on to the ledge like a fish being landed in a boat. He was tied on to a belay beside Jim and it was Abi's turn. She soon showed she was a natural climber by swarming up the rock almost as quickly as Jim could take the rope in. Jim tied her on to the ledge and set off up the next rock pitch. When it came to his turn again, Philip climbed with a lot more confidence and obviously enjoyed himself, even though he could look down a very long way to the cars moving slowly up Honister Pass. The three figures became tiny specks as they climbed higher up the crag and I finally lost sight of them among the jumble of buttresses and gullies. Over an hour passed before they scrambled down an easy gully and we collected Thor and returned to the Youth Hostel.

'Well, what was it like?' I asked, as we helped to carry Jim's ropes down to his van.

'Fabulous, really fabulous,' breathed Philip, his eyes glowing with pleasure. 'I was a bit scared when I started, but after the first pitch it was great.'

'Abi says she wants to be a mountain guide,' laughed Jim, 'but she won't believe me that the exams I had to pass are much more difficult than the ones she has at school.'

'But I can't understand why you have to pass silly exams to be a guide,' Abi grumbled.

'Think about it this way,' said Jim: 'if you flew in an aircraft you would expect the pilot to have passed exams to show that he was capable of taking the passengers safely from one place to another in all sorts of weather. Well, it's the same with a mountain guide. He takes people up rock faces or over mountains when they have probably never climbed before. The weather might be good or it might be a raging blizzard, but whatever it is, a guide has to make sure his party is safe. To be good at his job takes a lot of training and years of experience and, like any other job, to do it professionally you have to pass examinations.'

'Well, I still want to be a guide,' said Abi defiantly. 'And before I leave school I'll take guides' exams instead of "O" levels.'

'You'll make a good rock climber, I can tell you that,' smiled Jim, 'but one thing you must never do is to be tempted to climb on your own until you've had years and years of experience. 'Bye now, perhaps I'll meet you all again some day.'

Threatening clouds had been gathering all morning and, as Jim drove away a heavier shower poured out of the sky and sent us running for shelter behind a wooden hut. Sammy was nicely wedged in between us, but Thor stood out in the rain with water dripping off his nose like a leaking tap. He looked so miserable I gave him an extra large piece of mint cake and he chewed it slowly, pausing every few minutes to shake the rain off his back like a dog. Even in the shelter of the hut it was bitterly cold, and to warm us up I assembled the stove and heated a mixture of vegetable soup, spaghetti and corned beef. The shower increased to a heavy downpour and battered on the sides of the hut like a tidal wave. There was no question of moving on in such conditions and we huddled together and ate our soup.

'What's that building behind the Youth Hostel?' asked Philip, looking across to a long, stone shed.

'It belongs to the Honister Slate Company,' I said. 'They bring the blocks of slate down from the mine to be cut into lengths on special saws.'

'Someone must be working there now,' said Abi, 'there are lots of lights on. Do you think they would let us look round.'

'Well they have a show-room, we can take a look in there if you like.'

'Yes let's,' said Philip, 'it's freezing out here.'

We finished our soup and splashed through the rain to the show-room. The man in charge was very helpful and showed us how the stone was used for fireplaces, ornaments, paving stones and slates for house roofs. He told us that the mine had been in existence for hundreds of years and went deep into the ground under the very crag where Abi and Philip had been climbing.

'If you're really interested,' he said, 'I'll ask the

owner if he'll show you the machines cutting the blocks and how the roofing slates are made.'

The owner said he would be delighted to show us round, but Sammy would have to stay in his office. Sammy seemed quite content to lie in front of a warm stove and we left him and trooped into a workshop where a huge circular saw was slowly cutting through a block of slate.

'How does a saw cut slate?' bellowed Abi above the noise of the machine.

The owner switched it off and when it finally whirred to a halt he pointed to the edge of the blade. 'There's your answer — diamonds.'

Philip's eyes gleamed. 'Real diamonds. Gosh, it must be worth a lot of money.'

The owner smiled. 'Well they are diamonds, but not the type you would put in a diamond ring or crown. These are industrial diamonds, specially made for saw blades. They have to be well protected though and that's why a jet of water is sprayed on the blade as it cuts through the stone. I'll start this up then we'll move into the next shed.' He pressed a button and, with an ear-splitting whine, the saw continued its slow progress through the huge block.

We moved into a long shed where men were trimming different sizes of blocks for making fireplaces and ornamental fronts for buildings.

'What you have seen so far is all done by modern machinery,' said the owner, 'but follow me and I'll show you something that no machine will ever replace.'

He led the way to the far end of the shed where a man and a boy were sitting on stools with a block of slate between their knees. Each had a large hammer and a flat metal chisel and when they tapped the chisel on the block with the hammer a thin slate dropped off the

Abi tries her hand at cutting slates

block and was stacked in a neat pile.

'These chaps are riving roofing slates,' explained the owner. 'It looks easy, but believe me, it takes a lot of skill to judge where to put the chisel and rive off the same thickness of slate every time.'

The boy grinned at Abi and offered her his hammer and chisel. 'D'you want to try?'

Placing the chisel on the block he offered, she hit it hard with the hammer. Nothing happened. She hit it again. There was a loud crack and the block disintegrated into several lumps. The boy roared with laughter and Abi's face went red with embarrassment.

'Don't worry about it, lass,' said the man, patting her on the shoulder. 'He did the same often enough when he was learning and, in any case, the wee devil gave you a piece of stone that's too hard for cutting roofing slates.'

He demonstrated how it was done and when Abi tried again she managed to cut a slate. It was rather a thick slate, but at least it was in one piece and she was so pleased she wanted to take it home. Fortunately, I was able to persuade her that it would not fit in her rucksack. When Philip tried he could hardly believe his eyes when a perfect slate peeled off the block.

'You're a natural for the job,' laughed the man. 'I'll ask the owner to sign you on.'

When we had finished our tour the owner took us back to his office and presented us with a small block of polished slate each as a souvenir.

Outside it was still raining and a thick, grey mist hung round the mine buildings, turning the heaps of waste slate and the cranes into ghostly shapes. The owner had given us permission to follow a very steep road built by the mining company up the side of Fleetwith Pike, and it was like walking up a waterfall. Floods of water cascaded off the crags and swept down the gravel surface of the road, gouging deep furrows as it went. Swathed in our waterproofs, we were hot and sticky by the time we reached the top and we stopped to rest Thor and eat an orange. Thick mist hung everywhere and I worked out a compass course for Dubs Quarry, near the summit of Fleetwith Pike. Soon the rain-soaked, abandoned workings of the quarry appeared through the mist and we paused again while I worked out another course to join a path climbing up to Blackbeck Tarn on Haystacks. The rain increased and visibility was almost zero as we threaded our way through a maze of hillocks and outcrops of rock. Skirting a large expanse of bog, the path dipped down into a hollow and climbed obliquely across the fellside. There was no proper surface and a confusion of rocks and scree made it very tricky for Thor as he picked his way over it very slowly. In the mist we had little impression of height, but when a breeze sprang up and cleared it away briefly, we looked down a sheer precipice to Gatesgarth and the grey waters of Buttermere. Keeping a firm grip on Thor's lead rope, I steered him away from the edge and scrambled up to the safety of level ground beside Blackbeck Tarn.

Setting a course for Ennerdale, we ploughed through knee deep heather and quivering bog until we reached the head of Loft Beck and a slippery descent to Black Sail Hostel. Abi jumped up and down with excitement.

'We've completed a full circle,' she shouted. 'How far do you think we've walked since we started?'

'I'm not exactly sure,' I said, 'but it will be well over a hundred miles. Wait until we reach Gillerthwaite and, when we've had a hot bath and tea, we'll work it out.'

Philip stood in the rain, with water dripping off his anorak hood, staring at Great Gable. 'I can't believe we've nearly finished our journey,' he said sadly. 'It's going to be awful sleeping in a real bed.'

Thor's normal pace is slow, but as we walked through Ennerdale Forest we could hardly keep up with him. He knew he was close to home and he pounded along like a racehorse, whinnying for his friends, Lucy, Flash and Crystal. An answering whinny echoed across the valley and they charged over the fields to greet him, jumping ditches and kicking up clouds of spray from the wet grass. Thor longed to stop and tell them about his journey, but there was still some way to go to reach the house and I tugged on his lead rope to keep him moving.

We were soaked to the skin, tired and hungry, but

there was a smell of wood-smoke in the air and we knew we were almost at Gillerthwaite. When the house came into sight and Sammy heard Fang, my other dog, barking in the yard, he could not restrain himself a minute longer. With one bound he cleared the gate and ran for the kitchen and his dinner bowl. By the gate we paused to look back at the fells. The great crags glistened with water and masses of black clouds swirled and twisted round the peaks. A storm was approaching, but this time we could ignore it. The problems of gales and rain, rocky paths and treacherous bogs were over. We were home.

Journey's end — arriving at Gillerthwaite

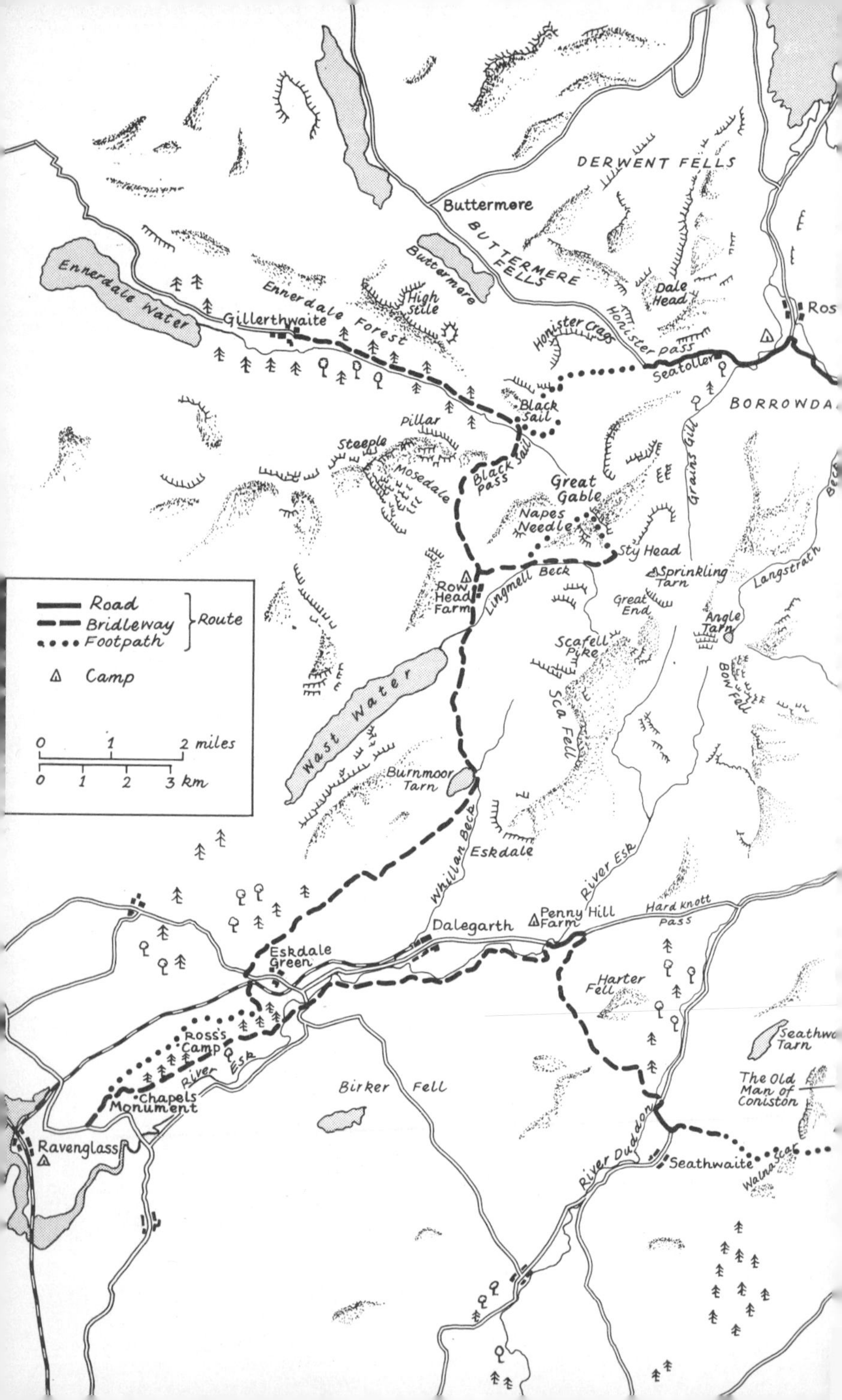

DERWENT FELLS
Buttermere
BUTTERMERE FELLS
Buttermere
Ennerdale Water
Ennerdale Forest
High Stile
Gillerthwaite
Honister Crags
Honister pass
Dale Head
Ros
Seatoller
BORROWDA
Black Sail
Pillar
Steeple
Black Sail Pass
Mosedale
Great Gable
Napes Needle
Sty Head
Grains Gill
Sprinkling Tarn
Langstrath
Row Head Farm
Lingmell Beck
Great End
Angle Tarn
Scafell Pike
Bow Fell
Sca Fell
Wast Water
Burnmoor Tarn
Whillan Beck
Eskdale
River Esk
Road
Bridleway
Footpath
Route
Camp
0 1 2 miles
0 1 2 3 km
Penny Hill Farm
Hard knott Pass
Dalegarth
Eskdale Green
Harter Fell
Ross's Camp
River Esk
Chapels Monument
Birker Fell
Seathwaite Tarn
The Old Man of Coniston
River Duddon
Seathwaite
Walna Scar
Ravenglass